A PRACTICAL PATH *to*

ENLIGHTENMENT

A Guide for Personal Growth in a Troubled Time

By Scott Elrod MD

to Stephen Engelberg MD

I am still paying it forward.

Table of Contents

Out of the Wilderness

In wilderness he did me guide,
And strange lands for me provide.
In fears and wants, through weal and woe,
As pilgrim, passed I to and fro...
William Bradford

They say that a butterfly can flap its wings in one part of the world and set off a chain of events that will result in a tornado somewhere else. My metaphorical wings can be no bigger than a butterfly's, but they are about to flap. Maybe a tornado... Maybe they will just get tired... Maybe I will arouse a hungry frog. All I know is that they are going to flap!

I know I am no more significant than a butterfly. My voice has no herald. Mine is a voice crying in the wilderness. Literally. As I write this, I see wilderness all around me. I accept that I have none of the traditional credentials that might inspire you to grace me with your attention. And I also know that I could be off to a bad start. You could have been turned off by the reference to enlightenment; because the word feels antithetical to your beliefs, or out of concern that I've co-opted your beliefs. Or that bit about being practical; how much sizzle could possibly be in such steak?

If we let self-consciousness loose, it will stop everything. I won't do that. People have been asking me to do this for too long. There is too much that needs to be done.

So, off we go! Welcome! I have high hopes for you. I may not have all the credentials you may have come to expect but, just maybe, the wilderness has yielded an unexpected effect. Many cultures have myths involving a person's solitary journey into the wilderness. There seems to be a near universal sense that, on such a journey, one might not just travel through space, but to the center of their soul.   For many, even the word "wilderness" evokes anticipation of something awe inspiring – a call to the spirit; a place where one sees beyond normal boundaries, transcends limiting beliefs, soars to treasured wisdom. John Muir once said, "The clearest way into the Universe is through a forest wilderness."

Yet, the wilderness is a paradox. It is not just a temple to the spirit. It is a place to find a pure form of reality. Truth, there, is objective and empirical. The laws of thermodynamics are firmly enforced. Get on the wrong side of those laws, as hundreds do every year, and the judgement is swift and the punishment is merciless. A common group communication exercise asks the participants to imagine they have survived a wilderness plane crash. The members of the group are given a list of 15 items they are to imagine they have salvaged. They are instructed to rank the items in terms of their importance to continued survival. There are

1.3 billion possible answers. There is one right
answer.

If you cross two polarizing lenses, all light is
blocked out. The same is so often true with
opposing articles of faith. We get by, sort of, in our
civilized lives; hunkered down under a
bombardment of conflicting beliefs. In the
wilderness, the enemies of existence will not long
tolerate such conflict.

To be a psychiatrist, like I am, one must be
comfortable with something akin to the wilderness.
Like the shaman in our imaginings of the ancient
tribe, we live outside the village – closer to the
wilderness than the rest. It is a state of affairs that
suits both the villagers and the shaman. I live on
edge of my village. I can see it below me in the
valley. Behind me is my path to the wild.

Take any cohort today that is inclined to
draw a line separating "us" from "not us" and,
more often than not, the psychiatrist is outside that
line. My favorite example comes from a trip I took
several years ago, to visit a friend at an Ivy League
law school. At one point at a party, if viewed from
above, you could have seen me
(uncharacteristically) in the center of the room,
chatting comfortably with a cluster of law students.
The room would appear to be about half-full, with
the people evenly distributed. Then someone
asked what I did. The answer and… poof! It was
like turning on a light in a room full of cockroaches

(I suppose some might find that simile satisfyingly apt). In a moment, I was alone in the center of the room.

Those poor people! They had spent all their lives trying to prove that they were good enough. They were desperately concealing anything they thought was evidence they were not within a carefully made and highly burnished shell. They feared that the psychiatrist had x-ray vision.

My country faces a profound shortage of psychiatrists. A leading reason why medical students do not choose the specialty is the perception of a lack of standing, of lingering stigma – even amongst the other specialties. Those that *do* choose don't care about that – not enough anyway. They do not even need that tribe.
All psychiatrists are close to the wilderness. Me – especially so. I had peers at my residency program who were aghast that I would choose to practice in such a remote place; far away from the one village that would always take me in.

Of course, any voice in the wilderness with an inclination to speak, must aspire to be a figurative one – the singular voice that, over time, comes to be widely understood to reveal important truth.

But the voice may, instead, just float away on the wind. Too many may be inclined to wonder, "Who are you to think so much of yourself." Too many may aspire to shame the voice back in line and, in doing so, be relieved of the bother of reading further. Worst of *all*, there's that part about "enlightenment." Surely it means that what follows can be nothing more than an egotistical, self-indulgent polemic! I understand that it is quite bothersome to be promised something new and then be disappointed. Time is precious. Stick with the experts. Stick with the comfort of the familiar.

Or... can I persuade you to keep reading? It feels like it is worth the effort. I have been led to a life spent easing the suffering of others. With suffering, it seems like the more you see - the easier it becomes to see. There is so much. Richard Dawkins once said, "The total amount of suffering per year in the natural world is beyond all decent contemplating." The same holds true for all of us. With practice, the eye and ear become attuned to the sights and sounds of suffering – a heart murmur, a wheeze, a limp, or a tremor. Similarly, I have become attuned. When I watch such disparate things as the flow of discourse on social media; the way advertising manipulates with fear and shame; the anger in our politics; almost all reality TV and talk radio - the suffering is neon bright.

There is much rationalization and even lauding of suffering. Proust: "We are healed of a suffering only by experiencing it to the full." Aeschylus: "Wisdom comes through suffering." Keats: Do you not see how necessary a world of pains and troubles is to school an intelligence and make it a soul?" Dr. Leonard McCoy: "A little suffering is good for the soul."

That all *sounds* good (though one could wonder at the motivation: Inspire the weary? Comfort the frustrated? Shame the whiner?). The problem is that suffering is such an inefficient teacher. We don't put students into a room and say, "Okay now, go invent algebra (it will be painful, but you will thank me one day)." Why must the sufferer invent the solution rather than draw upon another's? Is it cheating?

Also, the quotes don't consider the possibility that the sufferer is not inclined to pursue the purposed benefits of their suffering, or whether the sufferer is even aware of their suffering. My father once told me, with perfect earnestness – and in the face of voluminous evidence to the contrary – that he quite possibly was "the most, well-adjusted person who had ever been born!"

I certainly would not ask you, if you had heart failure, to use your shortness of breath to nourish your soul. You should be justifiably grateful for the physician's ability to hear what you could not (a heart murmur?), see what you could not (a failing valve?) and do what you could not (a prescription? a surgery?). If this venture of mine is to lead anyone beyond the experience of their suffering, it must have something in it for those who want comfort; for those stuck in their misery and for those oblivious to their suffering. It must hear, see ... understand something that is not obvious. And it must ease their pain. And, apparently, it must lead to something like enlightenment.

Yeah. Okay. Let's go!

Let's start with a definition of what I mean by enlightenment. There seems to be a general sense that, for the Buddha, enlightenment meant the achievement of *perfect* understanding. What an exclusive club that must be! *Any* step that leads to improved understanding should be celebrated! I think that when *you* experience enlightenment, it will be a sensation: you will attain a new perspective and, in the moment, you will feel pleased. It will come somewhat unexpectedly and you will feel pleasantly surprised. And, at the risk of being too literal, you will feel lighter – a burden will be set down. It will come with each and every step.

This is the sort of stuff that psychotherapy is made of. If that does not strike you as inherently obvious, you could hardly be blamed. I remember what it was like, taking basic psychology courses in high school and college. Psychotherapy seemed like an impossible mishmash of contradictory theories; faith dressed up like science; a gobbledygook of jargon. Someone would modify a theory; another would tack on new parts, like a patch in a computer code; someone would take old ideas and make them new with new language; while another would throw out everything that came before and create something new from whole cloth. Even in my residency program I can remember, during a psychoanalytic theory lecture, an argument (an argument!?!) about whether a gun was a symbol for male or female genitalia!

It doesn't have to be so hard. We can boil all the confusion about psychotherapy down to something quite manageable and understandable. First of all, we use a conversation. Secondly, we are dealing with people at the level of their beliefs. Even the cognitive therapist, with his focus on thoughts, must address at least one fundamental shift in belief: "I need to get better thoughts."

The patient comes to me with a set of beliefs – a perspective. The perspective causes him or her to suffer. It must be that I have a different perspective. My perspective *must* be a closer representation of reality (it would be unethical to convince someone of a delusion) and, if adopted, lead to diminished suffering. Then you just need to know how to shift a perspective.

How does one change a belief? It has been amazing how often a patient has asked me that over the years. I find myself tempted to respond, "Have you never changed your mind about anything? How about Santa Claus?" While most do believe that they must have changed their mind about something, at some point; such is the pervasive discomfort with uncertainty and the corresponding relief that comes with almost any belief, that they cannot remember when.

None the less, the process is straightforward enough: 1. You need logic on your side. 2. You need to accumulate a lot of evidence ("Let's see – in the scenario you just described does the old belief fit better or the new one?") 3. You need to help a person understand why they cling to the old belief and help them let go. 4. You need to help a person understand what makes them uncomfortable about the new belief and help them overcome it.

Here is an example: Somebody who has been married a long time would be well served by divorce. They avoid coming to this belief because single life seems very uncertain and anxiety producing. Divorce would mean that the person comes to grip with feelings of grief for lost time and opportunity. The person may feel that a change confirms years of foolishness and may even imply that the person is unlovable. Change will come when, through conversation, the person gains enough confidence in their ability to be alone; when they have grieved what has been lost; and when self-esteem has been recovered.

Changing a belief is like a divorce.

At the risk of making things a little more complicated, let me come at it one other way. I think it is fair to say that, when we react to something, we would like that reaction to be adaptive. We would like it to serve our interests. Some beliefs make that impossible. They serve as greased railroad tracks between impulse and action. Changing a belief is like creating a switch in the track to a new line. First, you must identify the elements of the old belief that are challengeable assumptions. Second, you must establish the basis for such challenges. Third, you construct a new belief. Fourth, you mull over the now competing beliefs; evaluating their merits and weighing new evidence. Finally, the new track is established as the main line. The new belief takes hold and adaptive behavior becomes automatic.

Let me give you an example of this: Somebody makes a mistake. They have a belief that making a mistake is shameful and, automatically, they feel bad. They withdraw. When they are persuaded of the belief that mistakes are inevitable and valuable fuel for personal growth, the automatic reaction will be to feel much more sanguine. They keep going forward.

The cool thing is that, when we do this, our brains change along with our minds. All the challenging and assessing introduces contributions from the frontal lobes that were otherwise absent. Completely new interconnections between regions of the brain are formed – like a new rail system!

I remember a lawyer once expressing astonishment that the process of psychotherapy could be conceived in such straightforward and logical terms. He had assumed that if something had to do with psychiatry, it must necessarily be couched in "mushy" and "touchy-feely" ridden terms. I did promise that this would be practical.

Change requires motivation. The Buddha is thought to have said that, to become enlightened, one needs the same motivation as the man running towards a lake with his hair on fire. That is not true, but you must want to get to the lake. We always have our reasons for wanting to go forward and for hanging back. The therapist must work to tip the scales.

When I was in my training, I saw a book on the hospital library bookshelf that, for me, had an irresistible title – "If You Meet the Buddha on the Road, Kill Him!" (Sheldon B. Kopp). The book compared the process of psychotherapy to a pilgrimage. It encouraged the reader to see that pilgrimage as sacred – that one must find his *own* unique way "to the top of the mountain." The Buddha (representing any person who says, "I know the path – follow Me.") must be avoided.

Of course, if, instead of the Buddha, you meet a charlatan on the road, it *is* important to identify and avoid him. But this "uniqueness" thing is a specious demand on the would-be pilgrim. All paths must, necessarily, be unique, because every starting point and pilgrim must be unique. Mountain tops tend to be rather small places. Everybody up there can see each other. Some perspectives must be closer representations of reality than others and only very few can be the closest *and* the most useful. The Buddha was motivated by a wish to end suffering and that led him to enlightenment. I don't claim to be an expert on him, but I suspect our ideas overlap. I feel pretty good about my perspective. I don't expect you to just accept it, though. I'm happy to go to work on your motivation. But, seriously, you *don't* need to invent algebra.

I have not run across anything that delivers what I have in mind. There are lots of self-help books. It is very easy to find someone's pet perspective. You can find something too esoteric to understand; something presented for consumption from an expert without regard for whether you are inclined to consume it; something rendered kitschy in an attempt to make it consumable; or something that contributes, without much context, a piece of a more useful whole.

In medical school, I was taught the adage, "Whenever there are many cures there are no cures." Take weight loss. There is no end to the diets, gadgets, exercise programs, supplements and infomercials you can find. And they will keep coming – until one of them works. Similarly, just on the subject of "self-esteem," Amazon has 16,000 books they will sell you; the U.S. Library of Medicine has 93,500 scholarly articles you can search; and Google will serve you up 93 million hits. All the while, the *vast majority* of people hold fast to beliefs that are antithetical to an adaptive self-esteem!

I want to see "A Practical Path to Enlightenment" as a new kind of self-help book. Not one with a grander ambition, but one with a more useful perspective. A guide book, perhaps.

Before I end this chapter, I have decided to include a short list - for those who know they are suffering; or for those who do not, but might recognize themselves - of the sort of traits that might identify the sort of person I hope to help.

You might...

*Habitually criticize yourself or others.
*Compulsively look to others for signs of approval or condemnation.
*Have difficulty accepting, or noticing that you have flaws.
*Feel as though your personal value is constantly in flux.
*Habitually compare your accomplishments with those of others.
*Be uncomfortable with uncertainty or are rarely uncertain.
*Feel that the worst pain comes from being misunderstood.
*Be preoccupied by your appearance.
*Feel that some of your emotions or impulses are inherently bad.

*Find yourself repeatedly being exploited.
*Feel that you can never do enough.
*Always get mad at yourself when you make a mistake.
*Feel paralyzed by the possibility of making a mistake.
*Find you are intensely interested in the possibility of enlightenment.
*Find you could not possibly be less interested in the possibility of enlightenment!

Complexity

*Thus says the Lord: "Let not the wise man boast
in his wisdom"*
Jeremiah 9:23

I have heard it said many times, "The only reason people go into psychiatry is to solve their own problems." There is much to admire in such a belief. It limits the number of reasons to a very manageable number. It is a closed conclusion that relieves the believer of the burden of further speculation or the assimilation of new information. It furthermore relieves the believer of any anxiety that might result from leaving the question uncertain. The answer is cast in a shameful light and, to the extent that the believer finds no impulse to become a psychiatrist within themself, this is also comforting.

There is one problem. The belief cannot possibly be true. Indeed, it is untrue in a way that harms the believer.

Obviously, we can see that the belief is about as simplistic as it could possibly be. The full measure of how inaccurate it is would, first of all, require a full accounting of the potential complexity with which one could answer the question of why a person becomes a psychiatrist. I will try to provide a summary of what such an accounting would look like.

The closing value of the Dow Jones Industrial Average reflects far more than what happened on that day of trading. It was built upon the shoulders of every day that preceded it; on what happened on those days. Similarly, we could see that the events of every day of our lives contribute to the wealth of experience we may draw upon when we make a decision. Some events will have minute influence and some large (and some large and yet unrecognized). Each can nudge us towards or away from a particular choice. A full understanding would then, also, need to go, day by day, into the lives of all the people who exerted an influence upon us; to understand why they became influential. And then onto the lives of those who influenced them, and so on, for generations.

Next, we would need to explore the dynamics of influence. For example, there will be a particular interaction, always evolving, between biology and environment. I would never have been able to choose a career in psychiatry were it not for a fortuitous interaction (not recognized at the time!) between my immune system and the mononucleosis virus (the illness caused me to take an extra semester of college, which helped me become more a competitive medical school candidate). To fully understand a decision, therefore, we must work out our understanding of biology until we have exhausted the contributions of science. We could do something similar with our understanding of environment, taking into account the sciences of physics, ecology, and climatology (to name a few). Another dynamic element we would need to fully understand is how people influence each other. Finally, perhaps, we would need to explore all the dynamics of how an individual is influenced by culture. Of course, the lexicon of each dynamic will be different from the others.

We would not get very far into this exploration before we would encounter the complexity of abstraction. An emotion, for example, is not a thing – it is a concept. We could discover all of the known biology of what seems to contribute to the experience of emotion, but the word will still remain a placeholder for something that is experienced.

As we attempt to understand experience with greater accuracy, abstractions become increasingly complex and esoteric. Thus, you will bump into sentences like, "There are three basic personality types that result from shortcomings of mirroring self-object relationships." (Baker and Baker) or, "The paucity of autobiographical recall in the avoidantly attached children and their parents with a Dismissing Adult Attachment findings support the notion that certain aspects of their minds are functioning in a unique manner." (Siegel).

I could hardly blame you if, at this point, you found yourself quite put off by this exercise! Of course, it is impractical; way too complex and time consuming to be of any use. And, in the end, the absolute truth will elude us still. I forget (and couldn't find) the exact reference, but I remember either hearing or reading Garrison Keillor discuss his book "Lake Wobegon Days." In essence, he said that every attempt to write nonfiction will produce a fiction. At some point, one always runs out of information and ends up with what must be a limited perspective.

But I would encourage you not to throw the baby out with the bathwater! Remember how that original sentiment about psychiatrists was so very simple – so black-and-white – that a first grader could understand it. I frequently find that I must urge my patients to aspire to a perspective more complicated than that of a first grader. The frequency is a little unsettling, but understandable. Even Obi-Wan said, "Only a Sith deals in absolutes."!

Simple, black-and-white sentiments *are* harmful. They box us into a corner. If potentially important questions like, "Should I see a psychiatrist?" or, "Can I ever trust a psychiatrist?" come up; we might do well to hope that we will answer with adaptive flexibility. Such adaptive flexibility requires a belief with compromised, yet increased complexity. Without such a belief, the harm of the simple one is not limited to us. To the extent that we share such beliefs with others, they go out to the arena of competing beliefs where they may, virus-like, infect another.

I once met a pair of Viet Nam era vets. By their behavior, they were readily diagnosable with PTSD. They vehemently believed that signs of PTSD were "bad" and managed to convince themselves that not only did they not have such signs, but also that PTSD was not even a thing that existed. In doing so, they commit themselves to a series of decisions that lead to suffering. If they convince others of their belief, they will suffer too.

A patient once heard my encouragement to think in other than black-and-white terms and remarked, "I suppose you want me to think in terms of gray." Her tone sounded rather bleak. "No!" I responded, "I want you to think in Technicolor. I want you to have ultra-violet, infrared, x-rays and gamma rays. I want you to have the knowledge that light acts, simultaneously, like both a particle and a beam. I want you to bring everything that a thinking mind can do to the problems of your life!"

An amazing, wonderful thing happens when we reach mid-adolescence. Our brains go through a burst of maturation and we become capable of thinking in dramatically more abstract ways. New intricacies of meaning and new perceptions of the connections and interactions between things can be made apparent to us. But humans are like cheetahs. A cheetah must learn everything it needs to know to be a successful cheetah by watching its mother and modeling her behavior (as opposed to leopards, who must rely on instinct and invention). Very few of us invent algebra. For better or worse, we are dependent upon the models available to us to learn what we need to know to be successful humans. That is how we come to manage problems like frustration, disappointment, discouragement, uncertainty, assaults on our self-esteem, and how to delay gratification. And, they don't teach that stuff in school!

That's just it! Almost nobody teaches that kind of stuff. It's quite strange. I would think that most of us would trade almost all we know about math to become proficient in such subjects! If so, we would surely want a teacher that could distill, from the ocean of complexities liberated by our collective capacity for abstraction, a *version* of the truth that is the most useful, and teachable, to the most people.

I would like to offer you a case for how the influences in my life have shaped me into a candidate for the job. My hope is that the case will stand as a piece of self-reinforcing evidence – that you will find my assessment of the influences to hit an intriguing "sweet spot" of complexity.

I will start with my paternal grandfather. Don't worry, that doesn't mean this will be so very long. I recognize, though, that it may seem like a surprising place to start. You may not often use four generations of information to come to an understanding about yourself (maybe you will find yourself inspired to try to start!).

Anyway, what you need to know about him is that he had the blend of attributes necessary to lift him from a family farm in Indiana, to a law practice in a small town in South Dakota and, then, on to the governor's mansion. Then, a confluence of stubborn fiscal restraint and inadequate compensatory charisma (he insisted on obtaining stone for a new statehouse from another state because it was cheaper) cut off the arc of his rise at a disappointing zenith. One term and then back to small town law. It must be so disappointing and surprising: always up, up and up... then, no more.

It seems that a sort of mantel was passed to my grandfather. It was believed that he had all the ambition, skills, pedigree *and* charisma necessary to resume the upward arc and, thereby, erase the disappointment. But then, great misfortune intervened. When he was still a young man with a new family, he developed tuberculosis of the spine. He spent the middle third of his life in a body cast.

And so, the mantel was passed to my father. He felt it. But he was not cut out for the job. He was shy; socially awkward and socially tone deaf. He had little charisma. He tried for the pedigree – joined the airborne in WWII with the hope of becoming a hero – and wound up not a hero, but in the only division that suffered no battle casualties during the war. He therefore struggled mightily with a painful conundrum.

He eventually came up with a remarkable solution: fate had purposely leap-frogged him. Fate picked him to be a sort of regent, who kept things going until… I was ready. I listened to him espouse this theory and its implications for me for hours and hours when I was young.

He had such a profoundly uncomfortable reaction to the possibility of having a flaw that he swept the dreaded possibility from his mind. He maintained rigid notions of right and wrong and reality and needed to have them assimilated by his children. Here is an example: he believed that soaking his head in cold water at the end of a shower prevented the common cold and he got mad at me when I, already then a graduate from medical school, would not adopt the habit. Indeed, his need to maintain an image of reality that suited his needs was so great, that he was quite willing to lose his temper if it would help.

He compulsively examined everything for the possibility that it might cast him in less than ideal terms. Thus, if I ever came to him with a problem; such was his concern that a child with a problem suggested imperfect parenting, that he would produce *the* definitive solution before he even understood what the problem was. It became so frustrating that I abandoned him as a confidant when I was quite young.

He based his self-esteem on competency. If a task could be observed to be executed with enough of an appearance of flawlessness, he was all over it. He was a wonder at making things. If he knew anything about a sport, it would be the fundamentals that he would know best. How to it *right*. When we bought a canoe, he (we all!) adopted a way of paddling he was certain to be the most ergonomically efficient. I have never seen any culture in the paddling world paddle like we did. If there was ever a contest between us where I came out the winner – we never did *that* again.

With regard to self-discipline, he had ambivalence. I sense that he detested most forms of physical exertion. Chores were presented to me as punishment. And it seems not to have occurred to him that the tasks of competent parenting might include the fostering of self-discipline.

My mother was the product of misfortunes mostly unknown to me. Those misfortunes produced a woman nearly devoid of competency. It had to be. My father could not have born any competition. Her coping strategies for life were essentially limited to 1) find a scapegoat (children come in very handy for this); 2) anesthesia via alcohol, opiates or self-indulgent spending; 3) reveling in the incompetence of others. She, too, maintained an absolute denial of the possibility of having a flaw (really quite an astounding psychological feat!). She greeted most tasks associated with parenting with resentment or anger dyscontrol.

She insisted on bringing me up Catholic - full on catechism and everything. I'm sure she did it out of a sense of obligation and a fear of her parent's disapproval. Rarely has there been a more obvious campaign of sustained hypocrisy. I'm certain she never went to confession. I never heard her speak of the value or the meaning of religion in her own life. As soon as her parents died, she stopped going to Mass.

Together, these two offered two environmental elements that had significant impacts. There were plenty of opportunities to develop competencies – sports, Boy Scouts, target shooting, music (clarinet –ew) (though they tried to kill others – writing, independent thought). And they introduced me to the wilderness!

Let me now summarize what my genome contributes to the question at hand. My native intelligence was above average. My mind made associations relatively quickly. I certainly did not distinguish myself in any discipline in school. I have never been able to see pictures in my head. My temperament was decidedly shy. I have always been relatively short and stocky. I have a "youthful" (once "baby") face that was quick to flush. I have flat feet.

There is another trait that I think is at least partially innate, but I can't be sure: despite being shy, and, in time, quite inclined to be self-critical, I can remember always having a robust sense of confidence. Many children have an exaggerated sense of responsibility; but only a minority think and act on it with much creativity. I remember how, when I was 8 and facing tonsillectomy (including a night alone in the hospital), I, alone, worked out my strategy for how I was going to cope.

There are, of course, a tremendous number of additional objective observations that could be made about these three players and their environment, but we now have enough for the foundation of an understanding of the question at hand. To finish the job of making a case for why I was well prepared for this project, I just need to show how the various traits came to interact.

Even a very small child can sense when his or her parents are ambivalent about or incapable of providing for their needs. The problem, however, is that the child can't make very much sense of it. The limits of experience and the immaturity of the brain (the child *is* limited to black-and-white thinking) allow only two explanations for why this is happening: it is their fault or… it is my fault. Woe to the child who picks the former. He or she is condemned to seemingly endless despair. If, instead, it is *my* fault, then there is something that can be done about it. Given that the second option is so very preferable, we may possibly be biologically predisposed to pick it and to overestimate our responsibility and potency. Of course, parents can play a significant role in helping the child choose. You probably can see where my parents came down on the question.

Mixtures of the two choices are possible. This is what happened to me. I idealized much of what I saw in my father. I internalized some of his black-and-white views. I had some ability to be discriminating, however. I could totally write my mother off.   And perhaps, it was her profound hypocrisy, indifference and incompetence that helped me to be discriminating. Even the dimmest child would have found *not* blaming her to be very difficult.

To the extent that I blamed my self – in essence, believing that there must be something about me that caused the failures of my "caregivers"; that diminished my worthiness of their care – I developed a habit of scouring myself with self-criticism (criticism *was* the modelled approach for change after all). I believed that I could identify and eradicate the supposed shortcomings that negatively influenced my parents and, thereby, end my inevitable and perpetual state of insecurity.

My insecurity was enhanced by my parents frequent fighting. It was the most frightening thing

– to contemplate the destruction of that upon which you are utterly dependent, when there already seemed to be so little margin for error.

There was little margin for error… Many children from similar circumstances grow up to be quite obsessive. We are vigilant for everything and don't let anything slip by. It can be quite remarkable to witness: the dental hygienist who regularly finds signs that elude the dentist; the nurse who anticipates your need before you do; the fire inspector who never misses a clue. In effect, we have forever said to ourselves that we must catch everything. For us, everything becomes a plate – and it feels like that plate must be kept spinning if the terrible feeling of insecurity is ever going to go away.

Here is one shape that my obsessiveness took. I have always really, really wanted to do well (failure was not an option); but I generally never wanted to, or could, work all that hard at it (it's only been in the last 10 years that I have finally figured out how to enjoy something simply because it was difficult). The perhaps unexpected consequence: I'm remarkably good at prioritization. When I was a medical student, I studied less than most of my peers but got good grades. When I was a resident, I almost always got out of the hospital before my peers. Yet, I have every reason to believe that my patients did as well or better than theirs and a good part of the reason was that I could identify the most important things to be done and give those things the most attention.

This is not so unusual. There is a woman named Elizabeth Grace Saunders who writes for the Harvard Business Review. She bills herself as a "Time Coach." She teaches people how to do this. People pay for what came naturally to me.

I learn in a peculiar way. My inability to see things in my head plays a role in this (it would be so much easier to memorize if I could). The important part of a complex whole seems to jump out at me. To aid my memory and understanding, I automatically convert the jargon I see into useable metaphors and stories. Details can then find their place in the story like ornaments on a Christmas tree. I often make references to conversations that happened in psychotherapy weeks before a session that the patient does not remember.

Here is another shape my obsessiveness took: concern for how those around me are doing. While the rest of my family was forever roaming in a field of anger dyscontrol mines, I was quiet and observant. Without realizing it, I developed a habit of intervening, just in time, to diffuse a situation. Also, long ago, a desire emerged in me to be the person for others that I wished could have been there for me. I have frequently found myself championing the weak. This includes the 15 years I spent as the medical director of a public mental health clinic.

I have also been suspicious of authority. There was a time (maybe it is still true – I haven't been there in a while) when you could walk down the hall of the residency office where I trained and see a framed photo of every chief resident in the history of the program. That is, until you got to the year I was chief resident! The tradition was suspended, indefinitely. I suppose my championing against the exploitation of my fellows was too intemperate for certain tastes.

Our brains have a property called "plasticity". Basically, the more you ask your brain to do something, the more it will shift how it does things so that it can deliver what you want. This is why practice is important. People with this kind of obsessiveness are practicing all the time and don't even realize it.

As you have probably surmised, I was an unhappy child. More than that, I was an unhappy child with strong doubts that others would/could do anything about it. But I had faith in myself. I have been a long-time believer in personal improvement and transformation. When I was 9, after a disastrous first season of baseball, it seemed obvious to me that the pitcher and the catcher got to have all the fun. Being left handed ruled out catcher. In a notable exception to the "don't work hard" ethos, I spent hours and hours between seasons throwing at a strike zone made of ribbon. By the time my second season came, I could throw strikes better than any of my peers. I didn't become a psychiatrist to "figure myself out". I will never, can never, stop that process.

My doubts about others were enhanced by the remarkable reliability with which I was bullied. Dad made me have a crew cut like his (this was the late 60's – early 70's!) and I had to wear clunky shoes because of my feet (*never* PF Flyers!). My face would quickly flush when I sensed conflict. This didn't help! I was red meat to bullies.

I almost was on top of it though! But then, in the fourth grade, we moved and, Sisyphus-like, I was at the bottom of the hill again. It would feel like I would remain there until the end of high school.

I found great comfort in the wilderness. Alone, for me, was safe. I was blessed with lots of opportunities to be there. Being really "good at it" was straightforward.

It seems like I spent all of half an hour deciding on my undergraduate college. Mom pushed for a Catholic school. There was one in Montana with a good reputation for "premed". That sounded like just enough states away.

I have always loved science and history. They explain things. I recoil from the simplicity of black-and-white thinking. To me, such thinking feels too much like the oppression and random empathetic failures of my childhood. Perhaps it is the experience of being misunderstood that makes one want to understand.

I met my wife while in college. We always knew that, after my training was over, we would probably settle near one set of potential grandparents or the other. My in-laws - both wonderful people - lived near the Bob Marshall Wilderness. It was not a very difficult choice.

The process of becoming a very capable psychiatrist was not hard. Not easy, but not hard. It was like learning your first language. Perhaps you are tempted to see that as bragging? I assure you, I take no credit for it. I hope that I have already made it abundantly clear that it was/is the product of circumstance. It just is. I am equally comfortable telling you that there are a great number of things I am quite incapable of doing well.

With my patients, I quickly discovered that my habit of boiling very complex subjects down to stories with a manageable level of complexity served me well. They seemed to love how I would explain things to them. In time, I wrote out the little talks I would give about subjects like depression or panic disorder, so that they could share them with their families.

Perhaps the hardest part of the whole, long process that has brought me here, was the required dependency on others. Medical training is like an apprenticeship. Most of what you learn is taught from teacher to student. If you go to an institution like mine, that means hundreds of teachers. Since it was a research institution, not every teacher was placed with their ability to teach in mind; or even their inclination to be a decent representative of their species.

The most notable exception was my therapist. He was a true spiritual father and the very best teacher. He gained my trust like I was a wounded wild animal. He will never know how I have payed forward the debt I owe to him. We didn't "figure" me out, but I got on the right path. And, to the extent that I knew that the day would come when I would be more-or-less on my own, I had "hair on fire" motivation to make the most of the opportunity.

In Zen Buddhism they use koans to provoke the monk toward enlightenment. My therapist had a kind of koan for me. Over and over, he would say, "My, how you seem to be self-critical."

He was right. I had self-criticism down pat. In this domain I was no monk, I was master. My koan was subtle and confounding. It gently suggested that there was another way of being; that a human could exist without self-criticism.

It didn't take too long to figure out that this was a real Gordian knot. I also quickly figured out that this bastard was expecting me to invent algebra.* Thank goodness he did, because I might

36

not have believed it otherwise. And almost everything in this book springs from my efforts.

Where does that leave us? I have a passion for complexity tempered by efficiency. I have a calling to diminish suffering and confidence in my ability figure out how. I have been here, in the wilderness, for 25 years; driving myself to develop the necessary skills for this task. More than anything, I have dedicated myself to the development of a useful language about change. Research tells us that it takes about 10,000 hours of practice to get really good at something. I've put over 50,000 hours into this project. I have also been graced by what thousands of patients have taught me. The place, the perspective, the strengths, the weaknesses – all – have worked to my purpose. I have been hammered on an anvil, hardened in a forge, battle tested and am guaranteed to blow your mind!** But time is scarce. It's time that I do more. For you.

*Upon reflection, it has occurred to me that I never asked for the answer. Perhaps he was waiting to provide it. It is perhaps telling that I assumed that it was my responsibility to find the answer (and that he was wise enough to let me do it).

**I got carried away. The Queen lyric came to mind and I couldn't help it. No actual guarantee. Maybe your mind will just pop. Or make a pssst sound. I truly hope it's something.

Shame

What do you regard as most humane?
To spare someone shame.
Friedrich Nietzsche

If you know so little about cats,
You don't deserve to own a cat.
Anonymous internet Troll

Imagine you have been visited by the Ghost of Christmas Present. Near the end of his stay you notice two small children within his cloak – "wretched, object, frightful, hideous, miserable." When you ask about them he says, "The boy is shame and the girl is fear. Beware them both, and all of their degree, but most of all fear this boy."

Shame accounts for more suffering and more difficulty becoming enlightened than anything else. We live in a time when more people spend more time giving and receiving shame than ever. There is hardly a topic that avoids its touch (even cats). A Google search of news stories from just the last 24 hours found stories that connect shame to such disparate topics as: body image, selfies, the exercise habits of British Royalty, French Nazi collaborators, insurance fraud, British drinking behavior, Gitmo, holiday travel, hall of fame voting, re-gifting, butterflies, panhandling, calls for more shaming, refugees, Bindi Irwin, grief feelings, a cricket team in Zimbabwe and the Indianapolis Colts. Much advertising seeks to manipulate us by evoking shame (I once counted 12 consecutive TV commercials). I just saw one that labeled sitting as "the new smoking"!

You are harmed by shame. Shame stands between you and enlightenment. Why? Enlightenment requires that you look at yourself. You must know your beliefs before you can change them. You must become able to observe your automatic patterns of maladaptive behavior. Shame makes that so difficult that most of the energy of psychotherapy is expended in overcoming it.

If you were to find yourself in classic psychoanalysis you would be directed to observe your emerging thoughts (look at yourself) and then reveal them: "free association." The process is not free. The typical person will (to the extent that they can bear to look) notice a thought and then react with something like, "Oh my god! I could never say that! I will sound like such a horrible person." The therapy proceeds like a slow-motion seduction: the patient floats out a trial balloon - a low-value shame target - and the analyst responds in a way that settles the patient's anxiety. Then the patient thinks, "Hmm, that went okay - maybe, someday, I'll risk a higher value target."

These days a trendy psychotherapy tactic is called "Mindfulness Based Psychotherapy." It comes at the difficulty people have looking at themselves another way: it sneaks up on them. You would be taught to meditate. It starts out seemingly innocent: just observe your breath. And then it proceeds bit by bit until – "OMG! I'm looking at my thoughts!"

So much effort. Patient: "Here, look at this. This is pretty shameful, isn't it?" Therapist: "Nope. Here's why..." Over and over. Eventually, we could hope that it would dawn on the patient (if it's not explicitly said) that the core belief – *that shame is a valid and useful concept for understanding and conducting yourself* – is simply not true.

Oh, how I know that can be hard to swallow. But, please, let me try to coax you into setting that belief down. I am ready to do the work: provide a compelling logical argument, evidence, and address the issues that make us cling to the old and fear the new.

Of logical arguments, I have three. The first one requires that you believe that human beings have instincts. Is that hard? Let's make sure we agree on a definition: an inheritable impulse to act (or think) that doesn't involve reasoning. My cat will bury a felt mouse in her food bowl. An ancient ancestor of my cat benefitted from an impulse to hide food for a later day. My cat inherited that impulse. An instinct is like the software that comes preloaded on your computer.

Do humans have instincts? How about a survival instinct? We don't, when confronting our deaths go, "I'm not sure how I feel about this, I'm going to have to think about it for a while in order to make up my mind." Instead, we generally have an instant negative visceral reaction and think something like, "Oh, how horrible."

If you were a programmer of human minds a survival instinct would probably seem like a pretty good idea. You would not want your newborn to have to invent a tactical response to hunger. It's better that crying is pre-programmed in.

The thing is, the program never turns off. That is a fact that leads to a lot of consequences.

How would we go about making a survival instinct program? First of all, there would need to be an element that imparted a sense of *importance*. The newborn can't be hemming and hawing; "Are my needs important enough?" Indeed, to the extent that a survival instinct is a good idea, the stronger the sense of importance, the better.

Is there evidence that a robust sense of importance affects us throughout our lifetimes? When we are two (and "terrible") it is not just annoying to be denied, it is *outrageous*. When we are a bit older, it is so very common to be scolded for being too big for our britches. And are we not incorrigibly idealistic as teenagers? Robert Kennedy was right to say that we dream of things that never were and ask, "Why not?" For a long time, it has probably been good for our species to be instinctually dissatisfied with what we find and to feel that we *deserve* better. Otherwise, we would very likely still be living in caves and saying, "Oh well, what can you expect?"

Given the option of choosing, we wanted it to be that the Sun revolved around the Earth. Given the option of choosing, it has been disturbing to think that we share a common ancestor with apes.

We create art that we hope will last forever. Our favorite stories tend to be our own. We want our lives to have purpose. We create "Halls of Fame". Our lives are our ultimate sacrifices. We bury our dead with things they can't use. Our gods always have time for us.

Satisfied? Overkill? I hope I can proceed. Our survival instinct program needs another element: a sense of *potency*. We would not have our newborn wrestling with doubts. The world will bring enough reason to doubt. We would want our newborn armed with an automatic inertia for perseverance in the face of uncertainty. When we decided it was time for my son to learn to put himself to sleep, he was not happy about it. He had what, for a time, seemed like an eternal sense of confidence in the potency of his crying!

Is there evidence that a robust sense of potency affects us throughout our lifetimes? Ask any 4-year-old why mommy and daddy are getting a divorce and chances are extremely good that they will say, "It's my fault." We will endure the very worst relationships and sustain ourselves with the belief that we can change our partner (a belief that, paradoxically, can be so very hard to change!). We have a remarkable capacity for superstition. When I was playing baseball, I drove myself crazy until I decided, "It's bad luck to be superstitious." Patients I have known who have experienced random tragedy will find themselves going over the events that led up to it again and again for hours – they cannot believe that was not in their power to prevent such an event. To the extent that we let ourselves worry about climate change, one of the most common methods of self-soothing (apparently even for Bill Gates) is to conclude that somebody will just invent something that will make it go away.

My rocket scientist friend once said to me, "Every boy (it would be better to say "child" these days) in America has *that day* when it dawns on him that he is not going to be the President of the United States. Now, I don't think the phenomenon is *that* universal, but probably it is very common. And it speaks to the influence within the child that determined, before that day, that something astronomically unlikely was within the realm of the possible.

When we do find our limitations, we trust that our gods will make up the difference. When Cortez invaded Mexico the Aztecs had, at least at first, more than enough power to destroy him. Their fatal mistake was to waste time asking their gods to do it for them. In James Welch's book "Fools Crow," there is a very poignant part that depicts a Blackfoot Indian medicine man trying to ward off the coming of small pox with ritual. He tries harder and harder, with ever increasing attention to detail.

On a tablet unearthed at the site of an ancient Phoenician colony a magician threatens, in order to gain control over a demon, that he will pronounce the "unutterable name of god." It was a literary convention in the epic poems of the ancient Greeks to begin with a call to a goddess, to invoke her aid in telling the tale.

I find that my cat demonstrates instincts involving importance and potency. She will decide, for example, that 2:00 in the morning is a perfectly good time for everybody to get up out of bed. She will meow. She will nudge us. If ignored, she will pounce on us. She seems not to doubt for an instant that this wish of hers is more important than any we might have. She does not seem to doubt for an instant that she has the power to bend us to her will. Indeed, she gives herself the opportunity to test this hypothesis regarding her potency almost every night. Every time, her sole

44

reward is to get locked in the basement. The instinct is unshakable.

Importance and potency. In terms of basic survival, the more of it that's wired in, the better. That's why I think that our most basic instinct, our fundamental expectation of what we will find when we enter the world is… *perfection.*

At least 88 languages have a word for perfection. God said to Abraham, "Walk before me and be thou perfect." Jesus said, "Therefore you are to be perfect." Nirvana is said to be a state of perfect peace, freedom and enlightenment. The Buddha said, "We already have perfect compassion, perfect wisdom, perfect joy." The Koran tells of how "Allah will bring his light to perfection." In the cosmology of the Australian aborigines there is, on the Plain of Nullarbar, a "Land of Perfect Bliss".

We expect to be perfect; that everything should be perfect. We are in thrall to the idea of perfection: perfect game, perfect score, perfect season, perfect timing, perfect manners, perfect soul-mate, a more perfect union (more perfect?) perfect 10's, perfect skin, perfect teeth, perfect cheekbones. And what is it with abs: perfectly toned or perfectly chiseled? Lexus' pursuit of perfection is restless. Nike is chasing perfection while Absolut vodka is convinced they have it figured out. Patron tequila is simply perfect, but with Chanel, perfection has never been so simple.

I'm pretty sure that *now* is the perfect time to buy the perfect gift.

There is just one problem: *we aren't perfect.*

For as long as we have records of man's thoughts, we know that we have been wrestling with how to explain the disparity between our expectations of perfection and the reality we discover. We could have decided that our expectations were irrationally high. But that would have required our more primitive selves to understand the workings of instincts. Only then, could we decide that expecting to be perfect makes about as much sense as my cat burying a felt mouse in her food bowl. It would also require that, given a choice, we choose the humbler of the available options. As history shows, we are not terribly inclined to do that.

Without a consideration of instinct, we can have only one option. Shame has intervened to rob us of our birthright. The first written mention of The Garden of Eden and the fall of man is about 5500 years old. It is thought that oral traditions had brought the story forth from as far back as the stone-age. The notion of a paradise lost is considered one the most universal mythological themes.

And now we get right into the appeal of the old idea and the fear of the new. The loss of shame is the humbler position. We may have to give up the idea that we could be perfect.

Perfect would be so very hard. There are so many things humans can do. Singing, cooking, writing, weaving, tracking, throwing, igloo building, wire walking… To be even pretty good at any of these takes thousands of hours. We don't have time enough to be even pretty good at more than a few things. Tiger Woods – pretty good at golf – not so good at some other important things.

And, for so many things, we cannot practice at all. We get one shot. My daughter recently came home from college after being away a long time. It was a first for us. Of course, I could have wanted it to go perfectly – that we would interact in ways that were always pleasing and always effortless. I made mistakes. I'd do a few things different next time, except… there won't be a next time. Things will have changed. New variables will have been introduced.

There is a lot to be said for a little humility. The ancient Greeks were one culture that understood this. In the story of Sisyphus, the protagonist went about proclaiming himself to be cleverer than Zeus. He was punished for this by having to roll a giant bolder up a hill - only to have it role down the other side - over and over, for eternity. I know people with sincere aspirations for perfection. They are perpetually making to-do lists that they genuinely believe will lead them to the desired goal. They are perpetually disappointed.

Frequently, they dream at night of Sisyphus; having never actually heard of the myth.

We can never employ all potential virtues simultaneously (which is something I also see people expecting of themselves). We must make compromises. When my wife was driving me to the hospital with my first kidney stone she displayed a fealty to the virtue of conscientiousness that would have appealed to many, but definitely not me!

Possibly the strongest, though often unconscious, reason why people are so keen on perfection is out of the mistaken belief that it would be possible to be so good that one would become immune from criticism. If possible, I suppose it would be blissful, nirvana-like state. Unfortunately, it is impossible. There is not even a very strong correlation between our faults and the frequency with which we are criticized. Trolls are all around us. The Del Monte Company once decided to delete preparation instructions from its canned corn labels. They had so much angry protest mail (people went to the trouble to write letters!) that they had to restore the instructions: "place in saucepan; heat."

So much of what we want to shame is nothing more than the expression of personal preference. I'm taking a foreign language course on-line. There is a crowdsourcing board. Some posts try to be funny. Some people shame that.

Others shame the shamers. Most fights that people have are escalated by shame when, if seen as differences of personal preference, they could be resolved relatively easily through compromise.

I have found that the people who most strongly want to get away from criticism mostly use self-criticism to get there. This is the first tactic I utilized to solve my koan. I criticized myself every time I noticed I was being self-critical (in medicine they have a saying that, if all you have is a hammer, everything looks like a nail). What a conundrum!

So, good luck with that. It would be much easier to let go of beliefs about shame.

I have known people who have missed out on so much because of their relentless pursuit of perfection. Their minds are always projected to the future; projected on the to-do list of the day. They leave their houses with miss-matched socks (or worse) because they are never living in the moment. They can never experience gratitude for what they already have.

My second argument involves how we are initiated into the world of shame. Consider the perspective of the toddler. We are very small then. We have lots of energy and curiosity. We have no judgement. We are totally dependent on awe inspiring, omnipotent seeming giants for everything we need. I once caught my then 2-year-old daughter with her hand on the front doorknob and a look of serious intent in her eye. It was about 15 degrees outside. She was naked.

There are two strategies the parent can use to keep us safe. The first is "containment:" "No", "Don't", "Stop", "Come here and sit on my lap", car seats, play pens, childproof locks, gates etc. It works perfectly well. A child so protected will emerge into adulthood without any harm done. There is just one problem with this strategy. It is labor intensive. It is almost impossible to resist the urge to utilize the second strategy: "Stop that and shame on you for *wanting* to do it in the first place."

Let's return to the perspective of the child. We see giants. We know we are dependent upon them. They look so displeased with us. Could they decide to withdraw their love and support? Could they decide to cast us out? My parents would "joke" about taking me to "the used kid lot." Can you imagine that? I bet you can!

I once had a patient tell me, "I know that shame is real because I can feel it." But was she? Return to the child. We don't know *shame* yet. What we would be feeling is something much more like horror. "They could cast me out..."

The effect is the construction of something like an invisible dog fence. The child approaches the forbidden behavior. It experiences the onset of an unpleasant visceral reaction. It ceases the approach. We can label the visceral reaction "shame" but that is no proof that shame exists.

Humans can be strongly influenced by the labeling of others. Anthropologists have found that a person's first experience with marijuana is almost invariably unpleasant. What could account for its popularity? People rarely use pot for the first time by themselves. They use it with experienced "coaches" who help them relabel the experience (and, in doing so, they even change how it is experienced). What we want to call shame is better labeled as horror.

And then we become doomed to the belief that there is something within us that could very well make us unworthy of love and care. As we will see, that unnecessary belief then permeates and degrades all aspect of our life.

Oh, but then we grow up. And many of us discover what a pleasant and useful weapon shame is. We can form cliques and use it to debase others and, thereby, bolster our insecurities. We can use it to mount the moral high ground and dominate our enemies in arguments. We can find it in others and (somehow) use the observation to sustain our self-esteems. We can use it to control children (and societies). And so, like a virus, it sweeps through each successive generation, without hardly a soul challenging the assumption that shame has any validity as a concept.

We once believed the world was flat. The popularity of a belief has no necessary connection to its validity.

Here is my third argument. Could we logically establish that shame has validity as a concept? I think you would agree that it would have to go like this:

We find ourselves at a crossroad. There is a good choice to the left and a bad choice to the right. For it to be shameful to go to right, it would be necessary that we have all the skills, experience, beliefs (etc.) required to turn left and just didn't use them. They were there, within easy arm's length, but some shameful act of neglect (or something like that) kept us from using them.

Are we in agreement? Wouldn't it have to be like that? Great – because *that never happens.* I can't tell you of the thousands of times I have put that question to the test. It is *always* quite easy to identify a missing prerequisite thing, whenever someone tells me of a choice that they believe to be shameful.

I know where some resistance to this idea lies. It touches upon our hopes for free will – that at that crossroad, lacking what we need to turn left – we can still, somehow, pull what we need out of a hat. What an omnipotence wish! I'll have more to say about this later but, for now, consider this: the only way to be sure that we had everything we needed at the crossroad was to have been at *exactly* the same crossroad before – and turned left.

We can come up with such a simple two-choice example from the real world. I know a fellow who plays a lot of poker. His stumbling block is "to bet" vs. "to fold." He bets too much. He knows this. Knowing helps very little. He can't quite let go of the belief that folding is a sign of shameful weakness. Shame makes him lose. In my experience, shame is involved in most "right hand" turns. The missing prerequisite element is to lose the belief in shame. Ironic.

A child a little older than a toddler once joined his mother, my patient, in my office. Of course, he was inquisitive and energetic. Unfortunately, I have just about the worst office in the world for such a creature. There are all kinds of breakable, valuable things that also are the sort of things such a child would find fascinating. During the visit, he was allowed to roam. I'm not sure if I was more horrified by the roaming or by the fact that his mother said, maybe 30 times, "Stop that, you are being bad."

Bad... Really? In what universe could he have been logically expected to possess the self-discipline skills required to resist his impulses? It certainly must be that such a mother, so bereft of self-discipline in her parenting, could never have imparted such skills (even if it were developmentally possible). Imagine how many times that child will hear that he is bad during his childhood!

The belief in shameful shortcomings robs us of our ability to recognize the un-shameful ones (maybe "simple shortcomings"). This is important because we treat them entirely differently. With shameful shortcomings, we tend to criticize ourselves for a while and then put the whole business out of our minds. With simple shortcomings, we over-train. My daughter was a little slow to speak. A little longer and she would have gone to a speech pathologist (but then… speech flooded upon us!). No one would consider the slow onset of speech to be shameful (at the very least, not in the child). If she had gone to therapy, then she would have spent *a lot more time* working on speaking than her peers.

My favorite example of this involves an extended family in remote rural Turkey that walked on all fours, like bears. When scientists discovered them, as you can imagine, they had a field day. In time, it was discovered that they had a hereditable defect in their cerebellums (the part of the brain that manages balance). After making this discovery, the scientists decided to see if anything could be done to help the family walk more conventionally. Not too far away, they found a physical therapist, who helped them move in some rudimentary equipment. And it turned out that it was not very difficult to get them walking on two legs.

Which begs the question: the physical therapist had been around a long while; the equipment had been available; the cost of treatment was never prohibitive – why didn't the people take advantage of it all? They were too ashamed.

People worry that without shame they will run amok; that they will give into terrible impulses. They worry without evidence that they should. It's just that the territory beyond the invisible dog fence seems so alien. Tear down the dog fence and there is much that remains to guide our behavior. What desirable quality would we sacrifice if we lost shame? Would we not cooperate with others? Would we fail to be trustworthy, courteous, or kind? Would we not work hard? There are plenty of practical reasons to do these things. And it can be pleasant, and fun.

I know that there are plenty of people who seem shameless and who fail to have these desirable qualities. They will never be shamed into acquiring them. What they miss is the belief in the value of such things and the value of others. These beliefs can be instilled without shame.

I once asked a patient if he could think of any possible source of motivation that might move him should he abandon his obsessive pursuit of perfection. He looked at me, blankly, for minutes. Finally, I had to help him: "You could want your marriage to be happier. You could want your children to grow up well adjusted. You could want to be more financially secure. You could want to be more satisfied by your work." These don't need to be moral issues. The practicality of them is impulse enough.

We are often taught that shame is the compass that should guide us. We are not taught that *wanting* is a good compass – that we could want good things and have good judgement about what we want. Wanting sounds and feels too much like selfishness. Selfishness is supposed to be shameful. Oh dear, another idea for the dust bin.

There will be much more on this but, for now, imagine the classic selfishness shaming situation: the child won't share. Now, if that child could think in a sophisticated way, like we can, we could say to him: "You know… that other child has a bunch of toys that you don't have. If you share this one toy, you will probably get access to all those toys."

Sharing would be the wiser form of selfishness. That is, unless the other child doesn't allow access to the toys. Then we may want to re-evaluate the frequency with which such playdates take place! Wisdom is the key that makes *wanting* the good compass.

Some people feel that shame is essential for the maintenance of social order. There certainly are cultures where shame is used to maintain conformity. As you might imagine, I'm not a huge fan of conformity. It tends to inhibit innovation and the quality decisions that come from diverse perspectives. In such cultures, the circumstances worthy of shame still must be determined. In many cases, the determination is made by a tyrant wanting to keep his subjects docile. The Chinese emperor who began building the Great Wall, ordered that almost all books be burned, so that he alone could determine cultural norms. The first samurai who lost face and committed suicide did so because he failed to gratify the wishes of his warlord. The state of shame that brings conformity within a culture is the same that brings war between different cultures. Some tyrants use hatred to control their people. The outcomes are similar.

You would think that a culture that thinks in terms of yin and yang would sense that the wish to use shame to serve its wishes could very well bring the opposite. Sophocles, writing almost 2,500 years ago, tells a tale of a king who tries to use shame to promote social order. This leads to a chain of events such that, in the end, the king loses everything that is dear to him. In "The Scarlet Letter" the Puritans expected that shame would bring conformity. For Hester Prynne, it had exactly the opposite effect: she began to think for herself.

With shame, it's a wonder we accomplish anything. It sets up the worst possible reinforcement environment. If *perfect* is the minimum acceptable standard, then everything below that line is experienced as a gradation of shame. What reward can be experienced with an incremental step of improvement? This is like trying to train your dog by kicking it a little less every time it gets a little better at doing what you want. Without shame, we must conclude that it *makes sense* that we are where we are. From this standpoint, we can genuinely enjoy incremental improvement.

It makes sense. Do you remember the story I told in Chapter 2? It makes sense that I am where I am. When I was coaching soccer I pushed for a belief that some find radical: every player is playing the very best they can at every moment in time – under the circumstances. The coach's responsibility is to figure out the circumstances. Perhaps there is a problem with conditioning, or technical skill, or tactical knowledge, or motivation, or cooperation. The coach then devises an intervention to address the problem. Circumstances are objective. Such coaches never have reason to be mad at their players.

Objectivity leads to understanding. Subjectivity, the stuff of shame, does not. I once saw a fellow drinking a Red Bull. I had never tried a Red Bull. I was confident that there was nothing in the name that suggested what it tasted like. So, curious, I asked him. He said, "It tastes like shit." I'm pretty sure that I did not receive information that increased my understanding.

This is the centerpiece of how I solved my koan. It dawned on me one day that, with every situation, one could obtain objective information – for as long as one wanted – for the construction of an increasingly complex narrative of understanding for why the situation happened. As soon as one introduced a good/bad, black/white, subjective element into the process – the process dies. From that moment on, I simply became disinterested in self-criticism. It's like riding a rocking horse. We feel like we are moving, but we aren't getting anywhere.

Perhaps the worst impact that shame can have on us is from what we can call "deflected shame." Certain parents refrain from shaming their child; but they lather it on thick everywhere else. The child gets the message that the very worst thing one can be is a target of shame. They will go so far as to convince themselves that they are perfect; completely devoid of shame.

Such people are completely dis-incentivized to look inward. They are groomed to look for scapegoats. They believe in shame, but, if there *were* any possible benefits to such beliefs, they are certainly immune to them. These can be the people that run amok.

A sad example is the story of the Trump family. Donald Trump's older brother, Fred Jr., died young at 43 after struggles with alcohol addiction. The family message was that it was all the product of something horribly shameful. So shameful, in fact, that Fred's children were largely cut out of their grandfather's will. Have you ever seen anybody more determined to be disassociated from the possibility of shame than the President?

Political parties generally cling to traditional scapegoats when explaining the worlds woes. Pundits have said that President Trump's electoral success rested largely on his remarkable capacity to break molds and find more scapegoats. We can only hope that the same forces that have led to fortunes from outward looking do not lead to inward blindness. The result can only be inflexible, maladaptive acts shackled to instinct.

But there are many, more benign forms of this problem. I have known many decent, well-intentioned people who struggle in life because of deflected shame. They try to guide themselves with admirable values. Nonetheless, they have perpetual troubles with interpersonal relationships and they can never fix them. *They can never look at the source.*

Let me end on a lighter note. The only Buddhist monk I have ever met was a jailhouse convert. He was covered in tattoos, had a loop earring and came to his appointments with a parrot on his shoulder. This pirate-monk (an underappreciated role-playing game character, perhaps?) lived in a Tibetan Buddhist monastery. At one appointment, the monk very excitedly told me of how he had solved the koan which asks the sound of one hand clapping (I have no idea why a

Tibetan Buddhist was trying to solve a Zen koan. Perhaps things are more ecumenical than one might suppose).

Imagine this fellow, kneeling before his wizened and dignified master. He then lifts his shirt and begins slapping his exposed and ample belly with maniacal enthusiasm!

Insecurity

The treefrog in the high pool in the mountain
cleft, had he been endowed with human
reasoning, on finding a cigarette butt in the
water might have said, "Here is an impossibility.
There is no tobacco hereabouts nor any paper.
Here is evidence of fire and there has been no fire.
This thing cannot fly nor crawl nor blow in the
wind. In fact, this thing cannot be and I will
deny it; for if I admit that this thing is here the
whole world of frogs is in danger, and from there
it is only one step to anti-frogcentricism." And
so that frog will for the rest of his life try to forget
that something that is, is.
John Steinbeck, "The Log from the Sea of Cortez"

One night, when I was near the end of my
residency training, I noticed a bothersome feeling –
insecurity. I wanted it to go away. And then, it
occurred to me that I had been to hundreds of
lectures, read numerous articles and books, had
many dozens of supervisors, had four years of
psychotherapy… and I couldn't think of a single
instance when a strategy for making it go away was
ever suggested. I thought I was doomed.

A lot of people believe that insecurity is a
bad thing, a shameful thing. I have come to believe

that it is not. If you believe that it is bad, I'd like to convince you otherwise.

Insecurity feels like weakness. Weakness is a bad thing. Weakness has just got to be shameful. Nope.

Weakness is a wonderful thing. Consider the creatures that are true examples of the rugged individualist, like the mountain lion. A mountain lion has everything it needs to get by. Humans have been around for a few hundred thousand years. We could have adopted the mountain lion way of life. We never have, because it would be stupid. We could never compete, one-on-one, with a mountain lion. Compared to mountain lions, we are pathetically weak – physical prowess-wise. In terms of the physical, about the only thing humans are particularly good at is long distance walking. If we want to compete with the mountain lion for what it eats, we had better hunt in cooperating packs; or maybe give up hunting altogether.

A human has the most brain cells it will ever have when it is two years old. It's a brilliant plan. Imagine that you are told to pack for a trip tomorrow. You are also told that the trip could be to anywhere on the planet. You would want to pack lots of stuff you ultimately would not need - maybe a swim suit, a parka, a tuxedo. This is how our brain works. It is set up so that it can adapt to a wide variety of circumstances in a wide variety of ways. It is only after it "discovers" where it *is* that it begins to specialize. In effect, the brain discards the stuff it packed that it does not need and focuses on the use of the stuff it does need.

And humans are so very capable of specialization (especially when not weighed down by the wish to be perfect). I can do something you can't and you can do something I can't. By cooperating we get more of what we want. It would make sense if everyone in a group purposely made themselves particularly weak in at least a domain or two to maximize the sense of affiliation with the group (imagine trying to sell that to the Marine Corp!). Research shows us that the strength of commitment to mutual support within a group correlates better with the quality of group performance than the qualities of the individuals in the group (imagine trying to sell that to the New York Yankees!).

We should be able to sell it to the Yankees. There are frequent examples, in sports, where a talented player is sent away and the team improves. He may have been a very good player, but he was a locker room cancer.

So often what is proved by research was known long before. Alexander Pope wrote:

Heav'n forming each other to depend,
A master, or a servant, or a friend,
Bids each on other for assistance call,
Till one man's weakness grows the strength of
all.

Take any love story that works for you and analyze it and you will see that it is the weaknesses in the characters that makes it work. We cannot say, "You complete me," if we believe we are already complete.

I strongly suspect that phobia of weakness is most common in the United States. This is because of the unique way it came into being. Relatively rugged individualists (who struggled to get along with others) in Europe self-selected themselves for its east coast. In time, out of that population, relatively rugged individualists self-selected themselves for a wave of movement west. And so on.

There are certain traits and perspectives that work well in the middle of nowhere on the Kansas prairie. Those traits don't work so well in civilizations. Our common vernacular is not kind to individuals so endowed. We call them assholes.

There is *something* to be said for strength. There is no doubt that it is a virtue. But remember, it's very hard to employ multiple virtues at once. We need to compromise. At least *sometimes*, compassion, for example, would be a virtue more profitably employed than strength.

If we all were rugged, individualistic islands unto ourselves with no needs of others, then we could not even comprehend compassion. Where would that leave us? From my perspective, the supply seems preciously short as it is.

So, let's set the black/white, good/bad perspective on weakness aside and begin to think about insecurity in a more useful way. It is very useful to think of insecurity as having two layers. One layer we can call *here and now* insecurity. It stems from the fact that we can't predict the future and we must make decisions with limited information. Bad stuff is waiting to happen to us. Mistakes are inevitable. There is only one way to get rid of this kind of insecurity – it would be to become *certain*.

Certainty is very probably not a desirable state. I'm pretty sure about this (as I am about everything else I'm writing), but I aspire to be open to any new information that might change my mind. Certainty equates to a closed mind. Nonetheless, it's very popular in some circles. There are many people who will sell it to you. Some people are made very anxious by uncertainty (insecurity) and look to certainty for relief. But what if you didn't think of insecurity as a shameful thing? How anxiety provoking would it be then? If you think about it, there is a much more rational case to be made for anxiety with certainty than with uncertainty. With certainty, you are going to be blindsided. It's just a matter of time and you will never see it coming.

Often, when I am talking with my patients about this topic, I will say, "You know, at this very moment, I am feeling insecure. In fact, I feel insecure all the time." They often find such a confession to be stunning. It seems like I just admitted to something that is extremely shameful. It also comes as a surprise because, when I say it, I am quite calm.

Come to think of it, as I write this, I am feeling insecure!

The only way I could avoid being insecure when I am with patients (or writing) would be to become certain. What could be more uncertain than the conduct of psychotherapy? My understanding of a patient, though often very good, cannot be perfect. At any moment, I have nearly infinite choices concerning what to say, how to say it, and when to say it.

Insecurity is so very useful to me when I am conducting psychotherapy. I can watch as it ebbs and flows within me and use it as a sort of meter that monitors my attunement with my patient. Certainty would invariably lead to disastrous choices. It would be like flying without instruments.

It is therefore unusual for me to "look" insecure. This is because the *look* is all about shame, not insecurity itself. And, as you know, shame is an invalid concept.

One reason that here and now insecurity is experienced as shameful is because it opens up the possibility of making a mistake. A mistake can be experienced as evidence of imperfection. A mistake can be experienced as shameful. Certainty can feel like a way to avoid making a mistake. Unfortunately, certainty is little more than the use of denial. It *increases* the likelihood of making mistakes. And certainty prevents us from learning from our mistakes. As Mark Twain once said, "It ain't what you don't know that gets you into trouble. It's what you know for sure that just ain't so."

Certainty made the Titanic sinkable. And, sadly, later it made her sister ship sinkable as well.

Perhaps physicians are especially trained to manage here and now insecurity. The invaluable tool we are taught is the "risk-benefit analysis." This is the foundation of all medical decisions (and could be the foundation of all decisions!) We can compare the likelihood and magnitude of the possible good outcomes of a decision with the likelihood and magnitude of the possible bad outcomes. If we get to 51 – 49 or better, we know what to do – play the odds and go with 51. It's much easier to have confidence that we have measured the potential risks and benefits than to have confidence predicting an individual outcome.

Every time I prescribe a medication there is a small chance that it will cause an allergic reaction. I suppose we could call that a mistake. It certainly is not a desirable outcome. But, if the risks and benefits of the decision were truly considered, this "mistake" cannot be shameful. Such *mistakes* act as self-correcting information. I now have a new and improved risk-benefit analysis tool. I learn from the mistake and, if I document it well, so can every clinician who encounters my patient in the future.

One example, where we can see use of certainty as a defense against shamefully experienced insecurity, is with new parents. New mothers will tell me that they feel like they are back in middle school. They experience their peers as extremely certain. They see their peers form cliques (and even leagues!) of likeminded people around issues concerning parenting and then, as much as possible, mow down any dissent with shame weapons.

What could be more uncertain than parenting? The child is unique. Its situation is unique. Wouldn't the use of insecurity as an aid to the maintenance of attunement be invaluable? Consider any example of a parenting mistake that you can think of and, more often than not, you will find that certainty is in the mix.

We can now segue to the other layer of insecurity. We can call it *primary* insecurity. It's probably safe to say that the more vulnerable we are, the more insecure we should feel. We are never more vulnerable than when we are small children. We are dependent on seemingly omnipotent giants for all our needs.

And what do we expect of these omnipotent giants? Perfection, of course. We expect to be able to do whatever we want, have whatever we want and *still be perfectly adored.* We expect nothing less than to be the omnipotent center of the universe.

If you think about it, this is, at first, what we often deliver. Babies mostly get what they want when they want it. In any family gathering it is the baby that is most likely to be the center of attention. I once went to a wedding. In attendance, besides the bride and groom, was one baby. As they say, this was the *bride's* day. And yet, as I observed the event, I found myself thinking that if you could track the subject of all the gazes and comments (uttered or thought), baby and bride would have had a close contest. The poor groom – a distant third!

What a terrible state of affairs we would have if the instinctual expectations of the child were indulged forever. Imagine Johnny or Jane, about to leave for college, with parents reacting with delighted approval to everything they do: "You drove the car through the neighbor's fence? That's so amazing!"

It must be, therefore, that there is an ideal, developmentally informed "glide path" for the withdrawal of approval (and how very valuable insecurity could be to help us keep to such a path!). But, if it is possible to be too slow with withdrawal of approval, it must also be possible to be too fast.

Research has shown that even a one year old has a developed sense for the willingness parents have for the provision of approval and care. If the level of willingness is less than the child is ready to handle, it must necessarily lead to feelings of insecurity – a primary insecurity.

If the withdrawal of approval is consistently too fast, this primary insecurity stays with us. It may accumulate, like a reservoir. When we encounter information that should tickle our here-and-now insecurity, it reverberates in our reservoir of primary insecurity. This is why the feeling can seem so intense.

As I have written before, the best explanation the child can come to about their parents is, "It's my fault." The omnipotence part of the perfection instinct could be expected to be a driver of this. Over time, the child will, semi-consciously, collect a lineup of character "suspects" that they believe bear the responsibility for why the parents were unwilling to provide for its needs: not smart enough; not pretty enough; not conscientious enough; not strong enough (of course) or… too angry, too selfish, too needy, too lazy; etc. etc. etc.

What is the poor child to do? Usually, the approach is two pronged. First of all, shame and criticize the suspects in the hope that this will make them go away. And why not? The omnipotent giants seem to believe in this approach. They have modeled it often enough. The hope is that, if the suspects can be made to go away, the parents will turn into the kind we have been hoping for. If we can just eliminate the suspects, we become worthy of approval.

The second prong seems logical, in a way: if we can't find approval at home, we look for it elsewhere. In fact, we may well look for it in everybody. We tell ourselves (semiconsciously) that if we can just find and maintain enough approval, then the terrible feeling of insecurity (primary insecurity) will finally go away.

This brings to mind so many famous people who can never seem to get enough: Oprah Winfrey, Mitt Romney, every Kardashian – they can seem to be so insatiably appetent. I suspect primary insecurity. I will never forget Michelle Kwan, after getting (only) a silver medal at the Olympics. In the interview, right after the result was known, she looked into the TV camera - at all of us - and, while crying profusely, wanted to know... could we still love her? The poor, poor woman.

Have you ever seen pictures of "Harlow's Monkeys"? You probably have. Beginning in the 1930s, Harlow conducted landmark experiments on early development. Baby monkeys were raised with surrogates. Some surrogates were covered in soft terry cloth that presumably provided a sense of safety. Others were made of wire mesh and only provided for nutritional needs. Monkeys raised with the terry cloth surrogates developed normally while monkeys raised with wire mesh surrogates developed poorly and became miserable. Fame, success, power – approval surrogates – are little more than wire mesh. They don't make insecurity go away, no matter how hard we cling to them.

The dual strategies of self-criticism and approval seeking (and the automatic behaviors they lead to) rest on three faulty and untested assumptions. The first is that the attitude of the parents had something to do with us. If you think about it, their attitudes were in place and firmly formed before we were ever born. Thousands of life experiences had shaped them so that they *had* to react to us the way they did. They couldn't hold back approval because it was never in their power to give it. If the mythical stork had delivered us to different parents, we would be the same, but our reception would most likely have been entirely different.

I have known a woman who might qualify as the kindest person I have ever met. She had two children. One she experienced as a kindred spirit and they got along great. Their temperaments, something determined by biology, matched. There was no such match with the other child. It was not enough for the mother to be kind. The second child was doomed, by a quirk of chromosomes, to wonder: "What is it about me?"

The second assumption is that it was ever in our power to influence our parents and turn them into the ones we wished for. We could maybe, in small ways, effect behavior on a day to day basis; but that is a far cry from real change. I hope that you can see that it is the instinct of omnipotence that drives this assumption. I have known people who have clung to this fantasy all the way to their parent's deathbed. They will speak of a wish for "closure" but what they want is so much more.

The last assumption is that we can learn something about our worthiness from the approval of other people. I know that, to many, it seems like we should be able to… but we can't. Let's see if I can prove it.

Let's start with a basic example. Imagine that I have placed a bowl of chocolate and a bowl of vanilla ice cream before you. Would you prefer one over the other? For the sake of the argument, let's say you choose chocolate. Have we just learned anything about the ice cream?

Of course, not. We just learned something about you. Maybe it's something about your taste buds. Maybe you have happy memories that involve chocolate ice cream. Should vanilla feel bad about this?

Let's try another example. I have had a few thousand patients. We could line them up, from the ones that hate my guts to the far left to the ones that think I walk on water to the far right (and I guarantee you that they both exist!). All the rest could take their places in between, depending on how they feel about me.

What a crazy emotional rollercoaster ride my life would be if my self-esteem rose and fell with everyone that walked through my office door. It helps to know that, all the while, I am the same person. I can't learn about my worthiness from my patients. It would be terrible if I tried. How could they ever believe I was acting on behalf of their needs if my ego was involved with their improvement; or with whether they like me? On the other hand, if I put away any notion that I can learn about myself and, instead, focus on what I can learn about the patient from their response to me, there is a gold mine of information to be had.

Let's take the person who hates my guts. As I learn about them, most of the time I will discover that I remind them of an authority figure from their past that treated them poorly. Something about me triggers a cubbyhole of understanding they have about the world and they can't resist putting me into it.

On the other hand, consider the person that thinks I walk on water. Typically, they have had the sort of life experiences that have led them to deal with anxiety by aligning themselves with an idealized other – a kind of supercharged, animated security blanket. The more I wonder about what I can learn about my patients from the way they react to me, the better I understand them; the better

I can anticipate their reactions; the better I empathize with them.

I had an experience that wonderfully illustrates just how little you can learn about yourself from others. It was an almost perfect experiment on the matter. Once I had back-to-back new patients that, in many ways, were remarkably similar. They were young women of nearly the same age. They had very similar symptom complaints. I wound up prescribing the same medication, at the same dose, to both. I reviewed the potential side effects with each of them and gave my usual advice that, should they experience any bothersome side effects, they could try managing this by decreasing their dose by half.

I had reason to believe that the first of the two women would have few side effects, because she had told me that she had been on the medicine before and that everything had gone well. Nonetheless, after taking the first dose, the woman called me in some distress. She was having bothersome side effects and she wondered if there was anything to be done about it. I tried to reassure her that the side effects were not medically dangerous, were likely to be transient, and again advised that she try halving the dose. If that did not make the medicine tolerable, I advised that she discontinue it altogether.

As luck would have it, I saw both women, one right after the other, one week after their first appointment. The first, the one who had called, announced that she was furious because I had been so insensitive to her terrible experience and that she never wanted to see me or take any sort of medicine ever again.

Remarkably, the second woman told of having almost exactly the same side effects. It appeared that the intensity of her side effects was the same as the first woman's. As you may imagine, I was, at that moment, particularly sensitized to such a situation.

Had the patient tried halving the dose?

No, she had stuck with the full dose.

"We could still cut it now if you want to."

"That's okay doc, I can hack it."

The first woman must have had life experiences that taught her to believe, "If you are going through tough times, people will let you down." She had a reservoir of anger in her that greatly sensitized her to *any* evidence that her suffering wasn't being taken seriously (so that she was blind to any evidence that it was!). By contrast, the second woman must have had life experiences that taught her, "If you are going through tough times, you have what it takes to persevere." The reaction of each was set in stone long before they ever met me.

There was no way I could learn anything about my worthiness from these experiences, especially my fundamental worthiness as a person.

In the event that the situation might be cause to wonder about my worthiness as a healer, it is still much better for me to look inwardly rather than outwardly: Did I listen carefully and conscientiously? Was I empathetically attuned? Did I have any emotional reactions that might have clouded my perception? Was my fund of knowledge reasonably up to date? To the extent that I have dispelled concerns about shame and am comfortable with my insecurity, these are easy questions to ask and I *do* ask them (and others like them) continuously. On the other hand, for the folks I know who believe that they have "suspects" within them and who look to others for approval as a means of managing insecurity, such inward looking questioning can be very difficult.

There was a point in my residency training where I felt like I had plenty of suspects within me and I was an ardent pursuer of approval. And so it was that a particular psychotherapy supervisor gave me fits. Whenever I presented a case he would tear me to pieces with criticism. And it seemed that the target was always moving. Just when I was sure I had one of his pet peeves covered, he would slam me with a new one. It was not hard for me to entertain doubts of ever achieving worthiness – either as a therapist or as a person.

When I brought this up with my therapist, this was his response: in almost an offhand manner, looking at nothing in particular (so very like him) he said, "Have you ever noticed how some people always need to be the smartest person in the room?"

Very soon afterward, I found a new supervisor. This guy treated me fantastically. Praise flowed from him. He seemed so happy in to see me and spend time with me. We would meet in a coffee shop and he would always buy. We would talk about our cases. I had all kinds of problems I was trying to sort out. After a while, it became apparent to me that he ever only had one problem – such and such patient was in love with him. Ohhh... I got it – some people need to be the most loved person in the room!

My therapist was so awesome. He would throw out the clue and let me figure out the rest. I don't know if he was like that with everyone, but I like to think that he understood that it was an approach that worked especially well for me. I liked the unstated expression of confidence. I wish that, similarly, I could write just the right book for you. I sometimes wish I could write ten versions of this book and have it accompanied by an algorithm that would lead the reader to the right version for them.

But, in that one sentence from my therapist, I was given a Rosetta Stone that would lead to the most valuable conclusion: you can't learn about yourself (especially your worthiness or *value*) from the subjective opinions of other people.

Deflected shame makes it seem like some of us *ought* to learn from the opinions of others. I once knew of a psychiatrist who only took care of inpatients. One day, a substitute psychiatrist rounded on the patients and, one by one, they asked him to take over their care. The regular psychiatrist had seemed so arrogant and uncaring. When given this feedback, the regular psychiatrist responded, "What can you expect? They're all crazy."

It was the inability to look inward that caused this. As we will see, this is what made the psychiatrist make unwise decisions about his interests. It is only after we are liberated from the grip of shame that we can take in useful information from others. But it is never information about our fundamental value.

Let me give you some examples of how much better life goes when we look at things this way. A man goes out one night with his wife. In the course of the evening she loses her keys. She blames him. He "rightly" judges this to be unfair and a fight ensues. Afterward, when the man tells me about it, I ask him to consider the possibility that his wife had early life experiences that taught her that losing things, especially important things like keys, was the most awful thing one could do. I asked him to imagine the necessary emotional turmoil that must have been roiling in her to produce such an irrational response. Finally, I asked if perhaps he could feel some compassion for his wife. These days, that couple rarely fights.

A man needs something from a County office. When he finds out that he can't get it he becomes incensed and berates the clerk. The clerk complains about this to me and clearly takes this and all the other criticism he hears personally. The clerk gives me just one clue about the offensive man: he had said something about being a wounded vet. It was all I needed.

I asked the clerk to consider the possibility that the veteran had had a military experience quite unlike the one he had expected: He hadn't expected to confront so much fear; hadn't expected to be injured; hadn't expected the outcome of the war to be so dissatisfying; hadn't expected that the majority of his countrymen would be so disinterested in him or his war; hadn't expected that the phrase, "thank you for your service" would become something infuriatingly trite; hadn't expected that he would keep paying and paying for his sacrifice long after his return home. Then, I asked if it was terribly hard to imagine such an individual feeling, intensely, like he deserved some compensatory good luck to offset all of his bad luck.

It is easier when we can hear anger as pain. The translation is usually available. When we do, it is so much easier to see how the anger has very little to do with us. Circumstances conspired to create the anger long before we were in the picture. Substitute ourselves with anybody else in the same circumstances and the outcome would be the same. If we keep this in mind, we are much more likely to respond to the anger in an adaptive way.

A couple has a repetitive fight: one of the couple will act like they are listening but, later, prove that they were not. The other takes this personally and flies into a rage. The one who does not listen has had early life experiences that encourage her to deal with emotions by "checking out". The other has had early life experiences that taught her to doubt she was worthy of attention. The anger causes more checking out. The checking out causes more anger. The only way out of this conundrum is to learn that you can't learn about your worthiness from another and to wonder what you can surmise about them from their behavior.

We cannot learn about our value from others. Equally important, when we try, we blind ourselves to the wealth of information available to us about others. I once spoke with a woman unhappy with her marriage. Her husband rarely initiated sex. She was certain that this must mean that she was unattractive to him. I then had the opportunity to speak with the husband. He revealed that it was impossible for him to gratify any wish for pleasure without shame. It didn't matter if he was experiencing a sunset, eating a steak or having sex. With every opportunity, he felt compelled to convert it to a test of competency. He cannot enjoy the steak; he must choose and/or prepare the steak better than before. You can imagine what a chore sex had become!

A shy young man with little in the way of dating success once told me of how he had recently had a very pleasant conversation with a woman over coffee. They had planned to meet again the next day, but then the man was stood up. He was sure that this was evidence that supported his belief that he was unlovable. I told him that the woman's behavior sounded a little "flaky" to me, but he insisted that there could be nothing wrong with his "flake radar". I then asked him to tell me what else he knew about the woman. It turned out that she had a Facebook page. And it turned out that the only thing ever posted on the page was selfies… just of herself… at least one very day. Maybe the flake radar *did* miss something!

The need for approval that our developmental paths drive into us, undermines us from the earliest of ages. Long ago I was told of research into the question of how children are taught things. We are talking about toddler aged children doing developmentally appropriate tasks; like stacking blocks. As it turns out, there are just three ways that parents "teach" such tasks. The first is to take the child's hands and make them do what we want. The second is to demonstrate what we want. The third is to encourage what we want with praise ("Put that block on the other. You did it! Hurray! Good! Now put the other block on those two. Good! Good! Hurray!").

As it turns out, the choice of strategy is culturally bound. In Africa, mothers are usually show-ers. They will stack the blocks and then put their hands in their laps. They will calmly, expressionlessly, wait. If the child struggles, they will show again.

It may come as no surprise that in the United States, mothers are praise-ers. What does surprise many is that one strategy is clearly the most effective: showing. Hands down.

How could this be? It must be that even a toddler knows that, for every thumb that is up, there is a thumb that can be down. There is an intrinsic, primary insecurity built into the process. It seems like a particularly cruel irony that, with so many children, we build up the importance of approval, only to withhold too much of it.

With the child that is shown how, there is a simple, clear positive reinforcement: the joy of discovery of what we can do. Success delights our expectation of omnipotence.

We can find ourselves driven to try to manage primary insecurity by accumulating *enough* approval from others. It never works. What we need to do instead is look within, review the lineup of suspects we find and, one by one, determine that they do not (did not) make us unworthy; that they do not make us bad. In the next few chapters I will identify some of "the usual suspects" and show why it must be so.

***

But first, I will take care of one potential suspect right away. You may be tempted to believe, from all I have written, that *wanting* approval or validation from others is *bad*. Oh, please! It would not be like me to suggest such a thing. As you will see, I never think of wanting as bad; we just want to be wise about it.

We can spend decades searching for enough validation to make our insecurity go away. It's like crossing the longest desert. We are so thirsty. We feel desperate. Desperate feels like weakness. Weakness is perceived as shameful. Shame drives the wish for approval into our unconscious where it works away at our decision making without our recognition. To the outside observer, it can seem like the only thing driving our decisions and yet we don't see it.

I was once with a patient who was very nervous about a job interview. At a fortunate moment, I suggested to her that she was "desperate" for the validation she expected to come if she got the job. She could (bravely) admit that the word "desperate" resonated within her. Then I asked her if my choice of word had come as a surprise to her. She said that it had. I asked her how she felt about the word. She said that she didn't like it; it felt connected to something shameful.

I suppose we could hope that unconscious wishes would lose power compared to conscious ones. The opposite is generally true. This is because the conscious ones all must compete with one another. I often ask patients to imagine they have a lifeboat. I ask them to put in all of their conscious wishes: maybe – to live in accordance with their values; to have an interesting and meaningful life; to be a good parent; to do good work and enjoy the benefits of that work – whatever. Then, I ask them to add in the wish to have validation from others. How well does it compete? In a true lifeboat situation, how many (if any) of the other wishes would you sacrifice to keep that wish. Most people say none (especially after they have heard what you have just read!). And forever after the now shame-free wish takes its rightful place amongst the other wishes. It's not a bad thing. It's a thing. It's not at all hard to be compassionate (and even experience some kinship) about it being in you.

As I said before, we can "feel" like shame is a real thing. The same can be said for feelings of insecurity. Beliefs can lead to automatic, maladaptive behavior choices. Beliefs about the emotional and visceral signals we receive from our bodies are examples of this. The patient with PTSD hears a car backfire and panics. The patient with social anxiety goes to a party and freezes up. In each case, the person is operating with the belief, "When I feel this way, I'm in big trouble!"

These beliefs can be attacked like all others. We can look for challengeable assumptions. We can develop alternative beliefs. We can examine the evidence.

For example, if we are the sort of person who feels insecure in social situations it is helpful to consider the layers of insecurity. The emotional and visceral signals we are getting were set up when we were very small and vulnerable. It may be that such signals are truly proportionate to the degree of danger we were exposed to *at that time*.

What we should pause to consider is: this is *not* that time. We are now adults. It may be disappointing to fail to make a social connection at a party, but it is hardly the end of the world. The signals are now out of proportion to reality.

Similarly, we might *feel* insecure when we are facing an uncertain future. If the feeling is intense, we can become convinced *something* legit is coming that accounts for it. Instead of merely being alert to the possibility, we become obsessively vigilant. Our mind races over the possibilities. We try to imagine all the worst that can happen.

By considering the two layers of insecurity, we can realize that most of what we are feeling is rooted in the past instead of looming in the future. We can then turn our coping energies toward the past. At the same time, we will be changing our beliefs about what the feeling means.

The more we practice the challenging, the data collecting and the comparing, the more we knock at the door of our frontal lobes. The more we invite the contribution of rational thought, the stronger the neural pathways to the frontal lobes will become. By this process we rebalance the activity of the brain. The emotional and visceral signals will attenuate to the point where it becomes easier and easier to make choices that are adaptive.

Our goal, as adults, could be to take up the slack we experienced with our parents. By working to shift our belief that we were responsible for our parent's attitudes towards us; by working to shift our belief that it was ever in our power to influence their behavior; and by exonerating our line-up of character suspects – we will gain power over the influence that primary insecurity has over us. We will become our own good parent.

Selfish

Manifest plainness
Embrace simplicity
Reduce selfishness
Have few desires
Lao Tzu

There is almost no word I can utter that more reliably evokes a negative visceral reaction than "selfish." Surely, selfishness belongs in our lineup of character suspects that made us unworthy of approval and care. Surely, selfishness is bad.

Of course, we could aspire to think about things in a more sophisticated way than the black-and-white thinking of a 5-year-old. We are born with an instinct that everything will be perfect. The instinct informs us that the things we want are the most important things. The program can never be turned off. Desire is something indelibly, profoundly and intimately woven into what it means to be human.

The Buddha is said to have been determined to put an end to man's suffering. He saw that much suffering came from wanting. His answer was then intuitive, I suppose: learn to want less. Learn to be less human.

There are certain qualities that tell us that wood is wood, stone is stone and bone is bone. Take one of those qualities away and the essence of the thing will be changed. What was wood can no longer be recognized as wood. So it is with selfishness. Take it away and what was human can no longer be said to be human. We are therefore left with two choices: all humans (including you and me) are despicable and bad or, we figure out how to get right with selfishness.

Why does selfishness get such a bad rap anyway? It is because we assume that the pursuit of our interests must come at the expense of someone else's. A boy goes to a birthday party. When the cake is served, he wants more than his fair share. For shame! Two brothers become billionaires. They create mountains of toxic waste in the process. Every year they spend millions of dollars trying to change laws so that it's easier for them to make even more money and easier to put the lives of poor people at risk. For shame!

It doesn't have to be this way. We can pursue all kinds of interests while simultaneously serving the interests of others. I will sometimes say to a patient, "You know, at this very moment, I am being very selfish. If I treat you with respect – it serves my interests. If I listen to you carefully – it serves my interests. If I say something that changes your life forever – it serves my interests."

It doesn't even matter what my interests are. The only things that can be judged are my behaviors. This is a key point that will be repeated. There is an incredibly important distinction to be made between an impulse and the behavior we choose to put it into action. An impulse is like a hand. We cannot make any judgement about a hand until it does something. Maybe it will pick your pocket. Maybe it will offer you a present. Maybe there will be a handshake.

The strange paradox is that, the more we like an impulse, the more likely it is that we will pick a behavior that *wisely* serves our interests. If the wanting of something becomes shameful, we fear to look at it. The impulse is driven into the unconscious, where it continues to influence our behavior.

The first person assigned to me to be a psychotherapy patient was a woman who had just recently been discharged from the hospital after having shot herself in the chest. When I met her, she was easily agitated and irritated. She gave me every reason to believe that she could be easily provoked to shoot herself again. I was terrified. I now know that I very much wished to never see that woman again. But, at the time, I experienced such a wish as shameful.

It came to pass that I misremembered the time for our next appointment by one hour. Not one hour early (of course), but one hour late. The woman was so angry about it that she determined that she never wanted to see me again! The unconscious wish had influenced my behavior. If the wish had not been shameful I would probably have had a very useful talk with my supervisor. That would have been a much wiser way to put the impulse into action.

A man came to me once after having had an affair. He very much wanted to save his marriage. He could not, for the life of him, come up with a reason for why he had the affair. He denied a need for attention or validation. He denied sexual frustration. He denied fears of his mortality and the limitations on opportunity it enforced. He insisted that, beforehand, he had always been driven to live a virtuous life. When asked what it was that had attracted him to the other woman, all he could come up with was that she seemed to need his help. This man was so blinded by shame that, even when acting in a way profoundly out of accordance with his best interests, all he could see was how he was acting "virtuously."

With extraordinarily few exceptions, our actions can be seen as serving our interests whether we recognize it or not. This is a useful viewpoint, because some people have such a negative, shaming view of selfishness that they refuse to acknowledge the presence of it within themselves. However, they can often accept this viewpoint on *actions*. Take gift buying, for example. Much can go into the choice of a gift. We can want to avoid bankrupting ourselves. We can want to demonstrate how important the relationship is to us. We can want to avoid the consequences of choosing a behavior that is outside of social norms (like not buying a gift). We can want to experience the joy someone obtains from our choice of gift. We may want to think of ourselves as virtuous, giving people. These wishes are *probably* in us, churning away on our decision process, whether we are conscious of them or not. What is certain is that we can easily measure the choice of gift in terms of how well it served these different interests.

Selfishness - *wanting* - is probably completely unavoidable. It's one of those basic logic rules that says that if something is an "always" it makes no sense to think of it as having an opposite. If the sky was always dark, it would make no sense to think of day.

Selfishness cannot be *bad* if there can be no *good* alternative. The Buddha *wanted* not to want. He *wanted* to escape suffering.

It would be so much better to aspire to be wise with our selfishness. Take the example above. There is so much that can go into gift buying, so many interests to serve. Often the interests are contrary and competing. The gift that provokes the most joy may be the one that most risks bankruptcy. The wisest gift buying behavior would need to represent a carefully considered compromise of our wishes. We might want a lot of practice with such potentially complex decisions. After all, it takes a lot of practice to be good at something (I was tempted to write "practice makes perfect!"). Maybe we ought to want to be very, very comfortable with wanting.

We would all be better off if, as a culture, we aspired to be wise about selfishness. Remember the science that shows that commitment to mutual support is necessary for groups to function well? We all have had enough experiences with groups that are dysfunctional to know that it would serve many of our interests if we act to promote good function. In the United States, it is said that its citizens have never been more polarized. Have its institutions ever been less functional?

Those poor Koch brother billionaires – suckling for all they are worth on a golden wire mesh monkey mother surrogate. If you watch them and compare them to the deportment of Bill Gates or Warren Buffet, they seem so much more uncomfortable, so much less happy. They have been less wise with their selfishness than their billionaire peers.

We may never be able to convince the Kochs of this. We certainly will not if we try to confront them with the "shame" of their actions. We will just become more polarized and entrenched. If we could ally ourselves with them - convince them that we are interested in their wellbeing - we could maybe have a dialogue about selfishness priorities. We could maybe convince them that it would serve their interests better if they were more concerned about the welfare of others. This is the sort of thing that is done in psychotherapy all the time.

***

I recently came across an article on the anatomy of apathy. It is amazing how much little strokes can teach us about the wiring of the brain. Apathy/ambition involves a number of circuits that go between the frontal cortex (the source of rational thought), through the limbic system (the source of emotion) and on to deeper, more primitive parts of the brain.

There appear to be three different, essential elements in the circuitry of ambition. First, we need an impetus; a spark; a "want to". Second, we need the ability to make sequential plans of action (step 1…step 2… step 3… etc.). Patients with schizophrenia are, for example, often very poor at this. Finally, we need to be able to bring joy to the process: pleasurable anticipation of the project achieved; self-satisfaction with the planning process; happiness and self-congratulation with the realization of the wish.

Little strokes can interrupt these circuits and the result is apathy and inactivity. It should be readily apparent that shame can disrupt the very same circuits. If it is not okay to want things; if we must always have perfect plans and perfect outcomes; if it is shamefully conceited to be self-satisfied – not too much is going to get done.

I once had a patient who complained of boredom. When I asked the young woman what she meant, the answer was so sad. When she was at home, she felt limited to activities she was obliged to do – a variety of chores. When she went out, she had two sorts of activities she could engage in: those that were obligations and those that would expose her to the critical judgement of others. Entirely absent from her life was the experience of *opportunity*. It is small wonder she was bored.

Obligation is a soul killer. Our spirit runs like an economy: give more than we get and we become depleted; depressed; empty. We have nothing left to give. The cure is opportunity. Almost everything experienced as an obligation can be turned into an opportunity. The more we can turn obligation into opportunity, the more we will have energy to devote to our interests. Wanting must be okay if we are going to see opportunities. I once had a patient whose best day in psychotherapy was when I convinced her that doing the laundry represented an opportunity: an opportunity for clean clothes and, after all, wearing clean clothes is so very pleasant!

I often ask patients to go through the following thought exercise: *Imagine you have won a trip to the Philippines. In short order you find yourself on a wide path winding through an amazing rain forest. Around one bend you see a beautiful butterfly. Around the next, there is a spectacular waterfall. Around the next, there is an amazing orchid. Can you imagine that you might find yourself moving faster and faster forward as you are filled with anticipation for what you might find next?*

Now imagine that it is 1942. It is the Bataan death march. You are on the same path, but there is a bayonet at your back. Can you imagine that there would be only one thought in your mind: "When do I get to stop?"

When wanting is bad; when selfishness is shameful; we kill the spirit in us that creates opportunity. Our lives become a death march of obligation.

The better we are at wanting the happier we will be. Difficult tasks will be ever so much easier if we *want* to do them instead of *have to* or *should* do them. I've never met anyone that exercised regularly because it was something they should do. I've met plenty that do it because they want to; because they are mindful of what is in it for them.

People can be afraid that if they liberate their *wanting* they will engage in nothing other than empty self-indulgence. It's as though we would choose the most fattening thing on the menu every time we went to a restaurant; as though we could never decide to want the benefits of healthier choices. The fact of the matter is that most self-indulgent eating is done by people living lives of obligation. It may be the only want that they indulge. It can be done quickly and secretively. It is rarely very satisfying, however, because it isn't done without shame.

When I talk to people about wanting, they often resist by pulling out their "trump card": the golden rule. We are *supposed* to do for others what we would want them to do for us. To these people, this is a rule of sacrifice and obligation. I see it as a rule of reciprocity. I must feel very deserving to even know what good treatment looks like. I will not let you exploit me, but I *will* be polite about it. And if you truly want giving to be your "thing," you had better take care to ensure that your tank is full. Of course, giving to people in need can often be a wise form of selfishness.

I am what they call a care *giver*. I am in perhaps the very best position to know how giving can lead to depletion. The only way I persevere is by spending at least as much time thinking about my own wishes and needs as I do about those of the patients I am treating. A lot of my work has been with other care givers who struggle with this.

I once met a recently retired man who had truly lived a life of obligation. He had always worked at jobs where he was told what to do. In social interactions, he always deferred to the preferences of others. He complained to me that he never felt like doing anything. When I suggested that we might work to identify and liberate his *wanting,* he looked at me as though I was speaking an incomprehensible language.

He described for me how he made a choice when reading a menu. He would notice a rich and savory item. **Instantly**, he would say to himself, "I can't choose that, it is fattening." He would then consider the salads. The salad choice felt like an obligation. It was not inspiring. He would then consider and reject another rich choice. Then, it was back to mulling over the salads. This would go on until the waiter came to the table and, feeling obliged to choose, he would choose on impulse.

When I suggested working on wanting, he was all for it. He wanted me to teach him to want to exercise; to want to do yard work; to want to diet. Basically, he just wanted to be better at doing what he felt he should be doing. He couldn't imagine that he could feel as though he deserved wants until he had mastered the shoulds.

Maybe we need to be able to walk before we can run. When I was little, there were very few foods I wanted to eat and probably none of them were especially health promoting. As I got older, the list came to feel restrictive and boring and, more and more, I developed a taste for other foods (I may be very old before kale and Brussel sprouts make the list!). I have found myself more and more interested in developing self-discipline around food choices.

This is also how I notice things work out with my patients. Some things are easier to want than others. I must encourage them to let it be okay to have their "dessert" before their vegetables. As they let go of shame and gain a stronger sense of worthiness, the list of things they are comfortable wanting grows and with it, their wisdom about it. The more energy they find in their tank, the more interested they become in wants that are a little more difficult to appreciate.

I once had a chronically depressed patient who insisted that the only thing she wanted was to lie in bed. I literally wrote her a prescription for "unlimited shame-free time in bed". The tricky part was the shame-free part. Spending time in bed can be a restorative thing, but only when it is shame-free.

I further suggested to the patient that she only get out of bed for an activity she truly wanted to do. Boredom, hunger, thirst or bladder are sure to intervene in such instances. Gradually, she found that she could diminish her shame about wanting and engage in life.

A lot of wanting can come at the expense of others. We must feel very worthy and comfortable with wanting to inconvenience another. We then must spend a lot of effort developing the ability to be assertive, so that we can get our share. Life is like a banquet where there is too little food to go around. It is not wise to aggressively hoard more than our share. But it is perhaps even less wise to stand at the doorway saying, "After you... After you..." We need to sharpen our elbows and get to the table!

We should want to be very wise about this. Too little consideration of others, and they will feel exploited. The relationship will be damaged. Too much, and the reverse happens. I find that this often comes up with new mothers. They feel obliged to give and give until they are depleted. Wise selfishness makes them better mothers.

In "Mansfield Park", Jane Austen writes, "Selfishness must be forgiven you know, because there is no hope of a cure." A writer aspiring for a pithy end to his chapter in defense of selfishness could be forgiven if he, at first, thought he had struck gold.

Unfortunately, the character who says this line is a classic Austen villain. She is terribly unwise with her selfishness. She demands that she be forgiven for her choices. She values wealth and self-indulgence over relationships. She is shallow and hollow and, of course, pays for it in the end. How foolish. Perhaps it's not such a disappointing quote after all.

Anger

Angry people are not always wise.
Jane Austen, "Pride and Prejudice"

A man can't eat anger for breakfast and sleep
with it at night and not suffer damage to his soul.
Garrison Keillor

Do you agree with Garrison Keillor? Most people do, including a lot of the all-time big thinkers. Plato, Einstein, Confucius, Seneca, Gandhi, Twain, the Dalai Lama, Emerson, Ben Franklin – just to name a few – were, definitely, not down with anger. Anger must be bad. And now, little nothing me is going to try to convince you otherwise.

Here is a mathematical equation for anger: what we hoped/expected to happen minus what did happen. We come into the world expecting perfection. Everything we experience in life that is south of that line will induce some measure of anger in us. Anger is inevitable and unavoidable. It is human. If there can be no non-anger state, it is not logical to think that the anger state is bad. We can do better than black-and-white thinking.

This is my favorite example of how very important it is to consider the distinction between a state of mind (anger in this case) and the behaviors we choose to put that state into action. We want to be wise about the behaviors we choose. We want those behaviors to serve our interests. For that to happen, we will need to take the shame out of anger, so that we can be very conscious of it. We must learn to like our anger. To the extent that feelings are so closely associated with our sense of identity, we will wind up liking ourselves better. Once we have learned to like our anger we will have eliminated one of the suspects from our line-up of unworthiness ("I am *too* angry").

Anger gets a bad rap because of low quality anger behavior choices. It is doubtless the case that some anger behaviors can be very destructive and maladaptive. I once had a patient who told me about how his mother, feeling she had been wronged, *burned the offender's house down*. When we are angry we have a broad spectrum of anger behaviors to choose from: from "burn down the house" at one end of the spectrum to "thank you, can I have another" at the other end. I hope we can agree that neither of these choices will serve our interests the significant majority of the time. It must be that there is a choice, away from these extremes, that will best serve our interests. Consider the act of writing a letter to somebody who has harmed you. Every single word chosen will shade the act toward one end of the spectrum or the other.

Deflected shame leads to many low quality anger behavior choices. The following "joke" demonstrates this well:

What do the spouses of wife-beaters have in common?

They don't know when to shut the hell up.

It's stunning that there are people (perhaps even some elected to high office) that would laugh at such a "joke". If they do, it is because they cannot look at themselves. They cannot take personal responsibility for their actions; because that would require that they consider the possibility that there is something they believe to be shameful within themselves. Such people almost never pick useful anger behaviors.

Often we have more than one interest we could want to serve with the choice of an anger behavior. They exist simultaneously and can even be contradictory. Simultaneous interests occur with all our impulses but it is possibly easiest to see this with anger. Here is a simple example: someone important to us has wronged us. We want redress but we also want to preserve the relationship. It could be very difficult to come up with the best compromise among the possible anger behavior choices. We could want to have a lot of creativity - and a lot of practice. We can only practice if we can sit comfortably with our anger and consider our options.

People often do not consider the fact that there are many pleasant, useful and adaptive anger behaviors. Indeed, the significant majority of the "good" things in our lives are the result of anger. Women get to vote now when once they didn't; buildings and cars are safer than they used to be; rights are better protected than they used to be (at least in some places); work conditions are better than they used to be (ditto) – all because somebody took the measure of their wishes against reality and determined that the status quo just wasn't good enough.

We may pick an anger behavior and somebody may tell us they don't like it. We will not have learned that anger is bad (or that we are bad). We will have learned something potentially very useful about the behavior preferences of the person. Later, we can use that knowledge to pick a more effective behavior; one that will better serve our interests. Lots of things can affect a person's behavior preferences. Italians, for example, seem to tolerate quite a wide range. Scandinavians, not so much.

Anger also gets a bad rap because we generally do not feel very serene when we experience it. We associate it with frightening displays of anger behavior witnessed in our past or with frightening ways we were shamed when we were angry in the past. Fear can be alloyed with anger and the distinction can be lost to us. But if we can get very confident in our ability to choose a wise anger behavior, the result is that anger can be experienced with more and more serenity. I often tell my patients that I am angry all the time (and so is poor Garrison Keillor), even at this very moment. Disappointing or frustrating things come to us in life as though by a conveyor belt. My anger about them will shift in and out of my consciousness, but it doesn't just go away. I am often not in a rush to pick my anger behaviors and picking one often isn't the first order of business at the moment. I am generally serene about the whole business.

The more serene we become with our own anger, the more serene we can become with the anger of others. This is helped by the belief that we can't learn about our value from other people. Anger behavior used to bother me a lot, but I've gotten better with it. If I am confident that I am not going to get physically hurt, I can watch the anger behavior in a dispassionate way. It's an opportunity to learn about the person.

Not long ago a patient called me a "prick" in the midst of quite a tirade. At the time, I briefly reflected on how long it had been since I had been called a prick (if ever!). I briefly reflected upon the possibility that I could have had a suppressed wish to be a prick and had provoked the patient. This seemed unlikely. A bit of a smile came to my face in response to the strange irony of the situation (I was trying to be helpful and seemed only to be a prick). This proved to be a somewhat unfortunate behavior choice (raging people hate it when they are forced to see the impotence of their rage behavior). Then I considered: 1) he became angry because he couldn't keep up with a question I had asked him; 2) the anger was bizarrely exaggerated; 3) it didn't fit the context (a person trying to be helpful asking a question so that he can do his job better) and 4) he had no insight about how odd his behavior was. These all suggested frontal lobe dysfunction. Armed with a new awareness of an emerging dementia, I could now pick useful, de-escalating behaviors specific to the situation. A few weeks later, psychological testing confirmed the diagnosis.

Anger can be jarring when it seems out of proportion to the circumstances that gave rise to it. Occasionally this happens because of dementia but, most of the time, it happens because of shame. Shame and a lack of teaching about anger lead us to process it poorly. This leads to a steadily accumulating pool, or reservoir, of anger within us. An incident can be thematically related to the reservoir and bring to us, in a flash, all of that accumulated anger emotion. For example, if we have been painfully misunderstood on numerous occasions, we can experience a flood of anger when we are misunderstood. We may act on impulse and lash out. We may pick a behavior that is proportionate to the reservoir and not to the moment.

If we take shame away from anger, we can look inward and begin to learn about our reservoirs and what taps into them. With practice, we can judge the anger within us for what belongs in the past and what belongs in the here and now. Then we can pick the anger behavior that best serves our interests – one that is proportionate to the circumstances (Perhaps: "You have misunderstood me [maybe because you are not very good at being understanding]. Let me restate my point."). We are going to want to feel very good about our anger if we are going to do this well.

We *can* do things to diminish the anger that is in us (I like to think of it as metabolizing the anger). It may serve our interests to do so.

Let's start with the mathematical formula for anger. It suggests three things we can do to metabolize it. First of all, we could look at what is happening. Apparently, it is short of our hopes/expectations. Perhaps we can pick an anger behavior that will get us more of what we wanted. If we get all of what we wanted, we won't have a reason to be angry. This recently happened between me and an insurance company. They had started a policy that I thought was unfair to me and my patients. I picked many anger behaviors. The insurance company changed its mind and ended the policy. Thank goodness for anger!

This is another reason why the last chapter was so important. If it is not okay to want something we will be hamstrung when it comes to anger behaviors. And we will lose one of the best tools for metabolizing anger.

The second thing we can do to metabolize anger is to consider the wishes/expectations. We could take a step back and question whether they were realistic. Where I live, the State Hospital for the treatment of mental illness is in a remote part of a rural state. I had to send patients there sometimes when I worked for the local, public, mental health clinic. I used to be infuriated by the quality of the care my patients would receive there. Then, one day, it occurred to me how hard it must be to recruit a psychiatrist to work in such a place. It reminded me of an anesthesiologist I met who had interviewed at a large inner city public hospital for a residency position. He had asked the interviewer what he looked for in a candidate. The answer: "The ability to speak English would be nice." From then on I experienced much more gratitude and much less anger over the treatment of my patients.

Our expectation of perfection gets in the way of this. Our world, like us, is incredibly mediocre, compromised and disappointing. It is unrealistic to expect anything more.

All of this informs the great wisdom of the serenity prayer. Sometimes we can make a change and sometimes we can't. It would be nice to know the difference.

This brings me to the last thing we can do to metabolize anger. There are times when we cannot do enough with behaviors or expectations to bridge the gap between wishes/expectations and what happens. Then, we can decide to grieve to the point of acceptance. We could have lots of practice with this. Life gives us plenty of, "You don't get to have that kind of life" experiences. Despite longstanding wishes, I won't ever get to be tall. I won't ever get to pitch in the Major Leagues. I won't ever have a metabolism that allows me to eat anything and stay thin. I won't ever get to hear the voice of a parent say, "I love you." This book may not be very influential. I'm going to die. Grieving is a great aid. Too bad we shame that too (more about this later).

I think there are two kinds of anger reservoirs. The first involves the "old stuff"- the painful, disappointing things from childhood. Having been habitually misunderstood and, worse yet, criticized based on the misunderstanding, is an example of this. Reservoirs are filled with the after-effects of the neglect and abuse and plain stupid parenting we received. We could want to get rid of such reservoirs (however, I am inclined to hold on to a bit of the one that sensitizes me to the behavior of bullies). To do so we must once again grieve. We must grieve for the loss of the arc our lives would have taken if we had been better treated. It helps, a lot, to have a therapist for this.

Our parents have a way of locking us into what we can think of as "reality battles." We are thinking to ourselves, "This is pretty messed up," and yet, all the while we are told, "No, no, this is good, this is normal." Before we can grieve we must resolve the reality battle. The therapist can act as the impartial "witness" to our experiences and help us come to a resolution about what happened and the reasonableness of our feelings about it. The stereotype of psychotherapy is that all you do is talk about the past. This is not true, but the job of reservoir draining can be very enlightening.

Patients often tell me they want help to forgive their parents. Usually they are motivated by what they think they should be doing. "All in good time," is the message I want to give. First we must see to the reality battle. First I must help them to forgive themselves.

The second reservoir is the more, "here and now" reservoir. When we do not like our anger; when we have trouble feeling worthy; we often wind up getting the short end of the stick in life. This causes anger which accumulates because we cannot generate the sort of assertiveness (anger) behaviors that it would take to get our fair share. As the anger level rises, we feel more and more uncomfortable with it and the likelihood that it will lead to undesirable behavior. Then, we give in even more. Learning to like our anger and what to do with it; changing our minds about our worthiness – these are the necessary things we must do to stem the rise of this pool.

There is an abstract idea that tries to capture an important aspect of our minds and how we come to make "here and now" reservoirs. It's called using a "reaction formation." It's a way of thinking about a maladaptive strategy (or defense mechanism) we might use when trying to manage an impulse, like anger, that we believe to be shameful. Here is my take on how to understand and make use of the concept:

Imagine life as a path stretching out before you. On this ideal path your relationships are all reciprocal; 50/50; fair. Accidentally veer into the country to the left of the path and you find that you are taking advantage of other people or are being cruel to them. Veer off to the right and you find that you are being a doormat.

Some people feel that, between the two accidents, the first is much worse. They can't stand the idea of ever being cruel to, or exploiting someone else. Indeed, this idea generates so much distress that the person lives his/her life, at least a little bit, out in doormat land. This gives them a margin for error so they never even accidently stray into forbidden territory. They are employing the defense mechanism we call reaction formation.

This perhaps would not be a troublesome thing if everyone did it. Perhaps we would only have difficulty getting through doors: "After you." "No, after you…"

The problem is that everyone does not do it. Some people are very happy living in exploitation land. They are like predators. They do not even see other people as people. They see them as objects to be used for their own purposes (if you are not a predator, this can be hard to wrap your head around). They are comfortable with exploitation of others. They will suck them dry. And they love, love, love doormats.

Sadly, it is hard to help the predators of the world. But my heart does go out to the doormat-ish types. It can be so hard to break out of these situations. First of all, maybe it's already apparent that the doormat's plan is designed to prevent the planner from experiencing the results of aggressive impulses. Typically, they have been raised by predator types and have been taught that aggressive impulses lead to horror (the best way to keep the predator's victim in a submissive state). Living in doormat land means that one is always getting the short end of the stick. The natural result of this is accumulating anger. The strategy allows for only one response to this: move farther into doormat land.

Predators are very good at what they do. When a potential victim beckons to them and says,

"Come here and join me on the 50/50 path", they are going to be angry. Their grand design is being frustrated. And so, they go to work trying to get the victim to go back to where they want them. The most common strategy used is to make claims that their intended victim is being cruel! I have had patients threaten that I will be the cause of all kinds of catastrophes if I do not bend to their will. They will lose their jobs. Their children will go hungry. They may even kill themselves. Oh my!

This is made more difficult because the reaction formation is operating on a mostly unconscious level. Almost every time I ask a patient using a reaction formation, "Do you want to hurt so-and-so?" they will categorically deny it.

"Really," I say, "after all they have done to you? I sure would. Not that I would, but I sure would want to!"

When I was in my training I had a patient who woke me up every night at 2am. She would claim that she was suicidal and that I had to say the comforting words that would keep her alive. My supervisor's first question to me, when he found out about this, was whether I wanted to hurt her. I quite earnestly assured him that, as someone eager to enter a caregiving profession, this was impossible. He helped me to see that wanting to help and wanting to hurt were not mutually exclusive impulses (like wanting and not wanting

114

to eat a doughnut!). And, oh yes, I did want to hurt her! She was driving me crazy!

What I learned is that the way out of the trap has two steps. First, we need to get more comfortable with anger and, secondly, we need to ask *reasonableness* questions. For, it can be that we want to hurt somebody. It can even be that we pick an action that someone perceives to be hurtful (or, at least tell us that it is) … and the action is still *reasonable*. Reasonableness must be the trump card.

Is it reasonable that I get enough rest so that I can do my job responsibly? When someone wants a medicine that I think will harm them, is it reasonable that I practice medicine in accordance with my values and say no? Is it reasonable that we have personal preferences for the type of people we have relationships with? Is it reasonable that we prefer those who would be pleased to be on the 50/50 line with us?

Is it necessary that everyone (especially the predators) agree with us that we are being reasonable? Obviously not!

It can be helpful to remember we only need to fight for our *half*. If, at the end of the argument, you can say, "look, I only want half", the other is left with three choices: accept that half is reasonable; reveal that they want more than half; or gaslight us with crazy talk about what constitutes "half". It's all useful information.

It's not so very hard to ask for half. Examples include: "I'm going to do such and such for our wellbeing for the next hour – would you do something comparable?" "I will happily do such and such on our upcoming vacation if you will do this for me." "It will be so good for our relationship if we compromise and meet in the middle on this."

And here is the one that I find I must encourage people to use the most: "I can see that you are upset, but I don't think it helps us when you treat me disrespectfully like that."

Some people will never want to let us have our half. They will be angry when we stick to our guns. It can be hard to have people out there in the world who are mad at us. But, if we want to live on the ideal, 50/50 line, it is mathematically necessary. If, when you put your head on your pillow at night, you can't think of anyone who is mad at you, you cannot be living on the line. Who knew that having a few people mad at you would be reason to sleep more peacefully!

Lazy

Hard work never hurt anybody.
Dr. James Manion

I am about to venture into dangerous territory. I am about to say something about the much-venerated dead. Because I will be carefully objective – and not effusively praising – it will seem jarring and maybe offensive to some. Dr. Manion came to Carroll College in Helena, Montana in 1956. You can easily find a newspaper article on the internet, from as far back as 1968, touting his ability to get students into medical school. By the time I met him, in 1980, he was something of a legend. He was "the man who would get you into medical school" and, given that it was a Catholic college, to speak less than positively of him seems, to many, tantamount to speaking ill of Jesus.

At first, I found him to be just about the most intimidating person I had ever met. He had the most impossibly deep set eyes that suggested the appearance of an animated skull. He had the scars from ancient and severe acne that made his skin seem reptilian. The quote above was from one of the last conversations we ever had – an argument – and that sentence was his final riposte.

150 students would start out in Dr. Manion's freshman zoology class proclaiming themselves to be "pre-med" (I have always found that to be a

pretentious conceit – and you will soon see why). The students were responsible to retain everything heard and seen in the lectures and in the accompanying lab. One year, a test question asked us to name the brand of microscope we had been using. In lab, much of the time was spent looking at stuff under a microscope. We had to draw pictures of what we saw. We had to use the most time-consuming method of illustration imaginable and we were graded on the quality of the pictures.

At the time, I would have considered myself somewhat lazy. But I worked hard in zoology. I put in more hours of study for one class than ever before. You needed 93% to get an A. I got 97% on the lecture tests (I think this was the highest average in the class). This was supposed to count for two thirds of the grade. I got 90% in the lab. I thought I was home free. I got a B. When I asked about it, Dr. Manion told me that it had been well publicized that you had to get an A in both lecture and lab to get an A. He lied.

Being, as I was, a person not especially inclined to work hard, but for whom failure was not an option, I know this for a fact. The line one had to cross to get an A was always brightly highlighted in my mind. I was a young man. Getting things from life besides an A was very important to me. I felt that any effort put towards getting an A beyond the standard was effort that must compete with everything else I could do with that energy.

"Hard work" whittled away at the 150 premed dreams. "Weeded" was the term that was used. In the end, out of the 150, only 18 applied to medical school and 16 got in. The percentage sounds good if you never think of the 132. It perhaps helps one to not think of them if one can think of them as not wanting to work hard - to think of them as lazy. 15 of the new doctors-to-be were the very best at devoting themselves to the assimilation and regurgitation of facts. Many of them were also among the most emotionally stunted and interpersonally inept people I have ever known. And then there was me, who studied efficiently more than exhaustively; who thought that future doctors might need a rich variety of life experiences; who had, based on that belief, a certain argument with Dr. Manion.

And what about Dr. Manion? He never did anything to encourage the dreams of the next 25 who might have kept their dreams alive if he had. His approach to teaching guaranteed that he would be teaching to the smallest number of students possible in the end. In a field that is constantly evolving, he taught from hand written (and barely legible) notes on acetate, yellowed with age, projected onto a screen. It could be asked, if laziness exists as a valid concept, just who *was* the lazy one in this picture?

Did all that work help me? Some. Perhaps it was overkill. I worked harder for 10 credits from one semester at Carroll than in any semester I spent at medical school.

There was a test we had to pass after our second year of medical school before we could go on. The first two years are mostly an exercise in fact assimilation concerning the basics of biology and the workings of the human body. Studies have looked at the question of whether high performance on this test predicts how well you will perform as a clinician in your residency. It does predict. It predicts you will do poorly. Hard work *can* hurt people.

Laziness doesn't figure into this story, however, because laziness doesn't exist. I know that goes against a lot of popular opinion. We have the opportunity to see lots of people struggling in life. Perhaps it's the beggar with the cardboard sign. Perhaps it's the person marching for a higher minimum wage. Perhaps it is the person who would have been a fine doctor if only a little more had been done to help them succeed in school. If we are experiencing relative success compared to such people, we might have to wrestle with uncomfortable guilt feelings. Or, we can banish away such feelings at one fell swoop. We can shame the misfortunate. We can call them lazy. Mitt Romney has had so many advantages that he had to do this to 47% of us.

There is a tremendous amount of complexity that goes into what we could be tempted to sum up with one shaming word. We could hope that many factors break in our favor if we are to possess industry and avoid this label.

Let's start with our genetic code. It influences our capacity for industry in a way that is set in stone before we are born. It is understood that we are born with basic temperaments. Some of us come out of the box with a "let's go" attitude, while others are imbued with more of an "I don't know... Maybe we should think about this" slant. The first is likely to lead to more industry. Both are of great importance to humans; especially if we consider ourselves as we have been for most of our history – living in small tribes. A variety of temperaments guarantees a richer and wiser consensus when decisions need to be made. After 9/11, there was very little trouble generating a feeling of consensus in America. It was often said that America had rarely been more "together". It's arguable that this did not lead to the wisest decisions.

Our genes also are the major determiner of our intelligence. I have known more than a few people who had trouble learning how to work hard because it was nearly impossible for their schools to find them something that was hard for them to do. On the other hand, intelligence makes it easier to do some things (the assimilation of facts, for example) and, for some, this creates the illusion of hard work because more work is getting done.

If we want to be able to work hard we probably want self-discipline, or the ability to delay gratification. Genetics could help here as well. Being a bit on the autistic spectrum, for example, could help. Such individuals often have a form of obsessiveness that allows for the repetition of mundane tasks. Charles Darwin spent thousands of hours dissecting earthworms. I wonder if he had biological help for such industry.

Or maybe we could want a healthy dose of primary insecurity so that we must keep every plate spinning and can never get enough praise (or money or whatever). Or we could hope to be the comparatively smaller and weaker brother of a first-born son (it would be best if the first-born dies). Such individuals can be fanatically driven to compete. Or maybe we could hope for a robust delusion that, with just a little more effort, we could be perfect. There is a lot we could wish to suffer through, if industry is the ultimate good.

If industry is our goal, then we should hope to avoid or overcome all the ill effects of childhood that would rob us of our sense of worthiness or the ability to be proud of ourselves. As we have seen, this good fortune is essential to the machinery of ambition.

To the extent that self-discipline enables hard work, we could hope that we are comfortable with wanting things. In my regular work, the most self-discipline requiring activity is the dictating of notes. It could be pure drudgery. When I am dictating, I put "wanting" to work in as many ways as possible. I try hard to turn what could be a dull obligation into an opportunity. First of all, I take pleasure in a good quality note. Secondly, I am quite practiced at efficient note making (shrink the un-fun experience!). Third, I like to throw in a phrase now and then that I flatter myself to think will make the transcriptionist chuckle. Finally, I pace around my office when I dictate so that I can be a little less sedentary and perhaps see something interesting outside.

We could also hope that nothing got in the way of a healthy comfort with our aggressiveness. Getting ahead is often a contact sport. Like I said, life truly is like a banquet where there is not enough food. To the extent that industry is valuable, it will serve our interests to have sharpened elbows that we are willing to use when necessary.

To avoid the lazy label, what we might want most of all is a good model; a parent (s) with good self-discipline to show us how it's done. I was never very faithful to regular exercise until my daughter showed an interest in becoming good at sports. I wanted to be a good model. I also modeled the ethic of extra practice and extra conditioning. I taught her ways of thinking that would make the misery of conditioning more bearable. We spent hours and hours on the field together. And this all begs the question: how many people get to have this?

I'm not anti-hard work. It has its utility. But the capacity for it depends upon many variables that are beyond the control of any individual we might want to call lazy.

There is more biology to consider as we age. Attention deficit disorders, depression and anxiety disorders work against self-discipline and industry. These problems run in families and have genetic underpinnings. There are many illnesses that also can have pernicious effects: chronic fatigue, hypothyroidism, sleep apnea, anemia, and Lyme disease, among many others.

I have known more than one adult who has cried and cried when they learned that they had ADD or when a psychological test revealed a learning disability. Their painful identity of being lazy, drilled into them by years of shaming, was shattered in a moment.

It might be that it is with laziness that I see the most resistance to the new belief and dear adherence to the old. This is because people who do not see themselves as lazy often use the comparison as a crutch for their self-esteems (how I know how they could hate the crutch metaphor!) They believe that hard work *entitles* a person to think of himself as superior to another. There can be an esprit de corps that goes with hard work; especially, hard work that leads to suffering. It is, for example, "the *few*, the *proud*, the Marines."

This is easily seen in the profession of medicine. I recently listened to a lecture given by Martin Samuels MD, who is a neurologist at the Harvard Medical School. His outlook embodied the group-think of many physicians I have known. He said that physicians should be very pleased to work long, hard hours. He suggested that their altruism and the prestige they receive should be enough to sustain them. This poor naïve man has the psychology backwards. He desperately needs to see himself as altruistic because, for him, wanting is a bad thing. But make no mistake, he wants something desperately: prestige. Suffering makes it okay for him to want it; it entitles him to take it. If you go to his website, you will see more badges of recognition than a petty dictator has medals on his chest.

Lance Armstrong and his team had great difficulty accepting that they were cheating. This is because the doping they were doing enabled them to make fuller use of their capacity for suffering (hard work). Because they believed they could work harder than others, they thought themselves superior to others. Cheating was inconsistent with the sense of superiority they had been so driven to create and so desperately wanted. The idea of cheating can find no purchase in such a mind.

Laziness would not be in our line-up of suspects for why we are unworthy of approval if we didn't have within us a wish for things to be easy; a wish to be at ease. Of course, we have this in us. We come into the world expecting everything to be perfect. We expect that all our wishes will be granted and, hopefully, without even having to ask. Indeed, we initially react with outrage when this fails to happen. The instinct can never be turned off.

Like with the other wants and wishes and impulses we have discussed thus far, there can be nothing *bad* about this impulse. We just want to be wise about what we do with it. All work and no play will make Jack a dull boy… and a bad doctor; and tired, irritable, cynical, naïve, and a host of other undesirable things. Cicero said, "He does not seem to me to be a free man who does not sometimes do nothing."

This seems like a good time to take a break from the review of character suspects and more directly take on the wish we can have to see ourselves as superior. It is a wish that can impede the path to enlightenment.

Free Will

Above all, he liked it that everything was one's
own fault. There was only oneself to blame.
Luck was a servant and not a master.
Ian Fleming, *"Casino Royal"*

Ian Fleming was writing about the game
Baccarat. It would be hard to find a game that is
more of a game of chance. One might as well flip a
coin. The only skill involves having the nerve (or
the foolishness) to bet and possibly lose all your
money. That is, unless you have a lot more money
than your opponent. Then the game is usually like
tetherball: tall man wins.

The writing is therefore testament to the
wish, as alive now as it was in the 1950's, to see
ourselves as the masters of our destiny. We want
to be credited for our successes. Of the available
options, it is not the humblest. It is steeped in the
perfection instinct. It can be extremely difficult to
shake. It cannot possibly be true.

Besides the fact that we want to, we feel as
though we have free will because we know what
it's like to have constrained will. If we want
something and are prevented from pursuing it, we
feel frustrated. If there is no constraint it feels like
we can say, "I wanted it and I went for it. It's all on
me." Perhaps... but the fly in the ointment involves
the question of *why* we wanted the thing in the first

place. The answer can be extremely complex and involves things we are either unaware of or have no control over, or both.

We can start at the atomic level. Ultimately, we are ruled by the laws of physics. The beat of our heart, the rumblings of our stomachs, the acuity of our vision, the firing of our neurons (the very number of neurons we possess) - everything - is subject to the laws of physics. We have no control over those. We might as well say that a rock has free will.

We don't get to pick our parents; the way their genetic material intermingled to make us; the country or time we were born in; our place in the birth order; or the influential people we meet along the way in life. We certainly had no control over the elements that made things influential in the ways they were.

Experience wields an influence over us all the time. Our bodies wield an influence over us all the time. Just having the ability to make a choice requires a delicate balance between our brain's processors of emotion and the processors of rational thought (the illness of obsessive-compulsive disorder is an example of how the system gets out of balance). We may make rational decisions or trust our gut, but we don't choose the process. The qualities of that rational thought will depend on genetics, nutrition and opportunities for modeling. And as we saw before, apathy and industry involve a complex biology in the brain and a complex psychology in the mind.

We have no control over any of this. We are often unconscious of most of it. Just because we don't feel a constraint; it doesn't mean it is not there. Some of us aren't free to be curious. Some of us have never had abstract constructs modeled for us. Such shackles bind firmly, yet are never seen.

I've known delusional people who were completely unaware of the fact that they held bizarre and impossible beliefs. I've seen neurotic people make the same mistake over and over again, hoping for a different outcome. I know of research that shows that the decisions of parole boards are influenced by hunger. All in these groups will believe they are acting with free will.

I can't see pictures in my head while my daughter sees them quite clearly. I am not free to think like she does and she is not free to think like I can. I will never be able to make decisions from the perspective of a tall person, a right-handed person, a black person or a homosexual – any more than I can choose to become any of those things.

It is a matter of lore that men think about sex every 7 seconds. That's probably an exaggeration, but how much control do we have over the frequency. We all know that if we are told, "Right now, don't think about sex," it will be the only thing we will think of.

Many thoughts come to us unbidden; as though out of the blue. I once locked my keys in my car. I spent many minutes actively trying to solve the puzzle of how to unlock my car without them. Finally, in despair, I went and sat under a tree. After about five minutes of not thinking about anything in particular, the answer suddenly just came to me. Patients will sometimes get lost in their thoughts while with me and say, "I forgot what I was going to say." I always say, "That's okay, it will come back to you." Usually, within a few minutes, it does and the chances are improved by my suggestion.

A certain smell or a song will evoke a memory in us. We have no control over this but such associations will always have an influence over our decisions. Advertisers depend on such things. Similarly, if we hear a new song or taste a new taste, we don't choose whether we like them. The factors that cause a preference were all present beforehand.

There is a whole host of research into the factors that influence our "gut reactions." There are a lot of them and they are all unconscious and largely beyond our control. Indeed, if science were the driver of our beliefs, we would have no choice but to conclude that the absence of free will is one of the most thoroughly proven truths!

An experiment in free will is happening at this very instant. If you never considered this question before; even if you don't wind up letting go of your belief in free will; you will never again be free to think of free will in the same way as you did at the beginning of the chapter. And, at the beginning, you were not free to think of it as you are now. Circumstances determine the menu of options available to us and the preference of the moment. So just where is the freedom?

In a fish trap, the fish senses ease of movement forward and constraint to the sides. It "chooses" to go forward. The trap offers the choice again and again. At some point the fish could be imagined to say, "It seemed like a good idea at the time." This is how we flow through life.

There are some out there who dedicate themselves to the task of proving that free will exists. The most common argument is that without free will, human beings would be utterly predictable, like machines. Everything would be "deterministic". They don't believe this is possible.

The thing is, despite the incredible complexities inherent in humans, they *are* incredibly predictable. A politician is going to give a speech tonight. We probably don't have to know too terribly much about him or her to be able to predict quite a lot of what they are going to say. My livelihood depends upon predictability. I am very careful about what I say during psychotherapy. I need to have a pretty good idea of how an interpretation is going to be received before it is said. A good deal of my mental energy goes to the creation of models that allow me to predict how my patients will react. I even often find myself making accurate predictions of the behavior of my patient's spouses, despite having never met them.

As we know all too well, weather isn't perfectly predictable. *Weather doesn't have free will.*

There are several reasons why we want free will to be real. We want the grandiose sensation that we are the masters of our destiny. We want to take credit for our successes. We want to be able to blame others for their failures and avoid taking any responsibility. We want to manage self-esteem by feeling superior to others. When harmed, we want to be able to act out our anger with vengeance. We want to preserve the pleasant fantasy that we could be perfect. We want the comforting certainty that comes from simplistic explanations. We want to keep shame alive.

Yeah, and we want to live forever. Wanting something to be true rarely provides evidence of the truth, but it may blind us to it.

There are so many advantages waiting for us if we let go of the wish for free will. First of all, consider the question of human value. There are only two ways to think about it and they are mutually exclusive: either we all have the same value all the time; or our value can change and different people can have different value. The latter depends on free will. The alternative is to believe that something else accounts for the differences we see in people: luck (you may prefer, "chance" or "fortune" or "circumstances"). When Bill Gates was in high school there was one high school in America that taught computer programming. People will tell me I am a good psychiatrist. I never take much interest in the compliment. To the extent that it is true, I am certain it is a state attributable to luck; quite a lot of it.

If there are objective reasons (luck) for why things turn out the way they do, then we can put our anger away. We can put our need for vengeance away. We can begin to experience more compassion. Perhaps especially, we can begin to experience more compassion for ourselves.

This is the basis of real grace. For many, forgiveness is a white knuckling affair that people engage in because they believe they are supposed to. This is not true of me. People have told me some of the most horrible things you can imagine. I am never judgmental. There are no white knuckles in it. It is always the case that an objective story tells of why things happened the way they did. Everybody is playing the very best they possibly can at every moment in time - under the circumstances.

This is also the basis for real self-esteem. If we can put away the need to be perfect or special, we can be satisfied with being unique. I wonder if you can imagine the weight that is lifted off us when we make this shift.

Think of any meeting you have been in. Consider how much of the energy at that meeting, directly or indirectly, went to no other purpose than self-esteem management. One person may be guarding turf. One may be scrutinizing the hierarchy of influence. One may be monitoring for any sign of disrespect or favoritism. One might be trying very hard to come across as intelligent. We would be much more effective and efficient if we didn't waste all that energy. People fear that without the motivation to be superior or special, we would all become apathetic dullards. The truth is the opposite. There will always be other passions and plenty of practical reasons to strive. With a real, humbler notion of self-esteem, it will all come so much easier.

Poor Stuart Smalley sits before a mirror spewing saccharine self-affirmations (if you are not old, like me, and don't know who I am talking about, you can still see him on YouTube). It always makes me throw up a little in my mouth. If we think we are a bad person, the alternative is not to fool ourselves into thinking we are a good person. The healthy alternative is to accept that we are just *a person*.

This is also the basis of real justice. If we could set aside our wish for vengeance and become curious about the circumstance that led to a criminal act, we could mete out justice much more wisely. Almost nobody is very happy with what we do now. We (in the United States) could hardly design a system that would be more expensive and more likely to increase recidivism than the one we have now. If we could know *why* an act happened, we could customize sentencing (would we even call it sentencing?) to maximize the chances that the act wouldn't be repeated. This doesn't mean we would set aside the need to protect society. We would be making choices that would increase the chances that society would be protected. It also doesn't mean that we must set aside our *distaste* for certain behavior. We can keep our personal preferences about behavior without having to label them as shameful (or willful).

Research shows that an individual's ability to accept responsibility for his actions (as opposed to blaming others) predicts a much lower rate of recidivism. Couldn't this be just one of many possible variables that we might consider when handing out justice? It certainly makes no sense to treat the person who can accept responsibility the same as the one who can't. Noticing the distinction could also lead us to consider how to increase the likelihood of accountability in people. It is very likely that it will be difficult in the individual. Maybe we should want to take on the culture. Shame will make this much more difficult. The wish for omnipotence will make this difficult. At the root of it all, the same forces that make us want to believe in free will, make us more likely to be criminals.

If you want to believe in free will, perhaps you jumped on the idea of "accepting responsibility". You may have thought, "How can anybody be expected to accept responsibility if there is no free will?" The sentiment confuses the states of shame and guilt. Guilt means, "I did wrong" (shame is, "I am bad"). A person can accept that they made a mistake even if they couldn't have avoided it. We perhaps should all want that for ourselves. How else could we hope to learn? Accepting that we make mistakes (that we are not perfect) is the only way to liberate the influence of the mistake so that we do not repeat it.

In *Moonraker*, M says to 007, "Somebody said that to be rich you have to be helped by a combination of remarkable circumstances and an unbroken run of luck. It certainly isn't only the qualities of people that makes them rich."

Resistance

*Everyone sees what you seem to be, few know
what you really are; and those few do not dare
take a stand against the general opinion.
Niccolo Machiavelli, "The Prince"*

I have now reached a point where I feel I
must address some potential sources of resistance
to the new. There are several reasons why we may
want to dig in our heels and say, "I don't want to
change!" "I don't like this path to enlightenment!"

1. Alone.

First of all, you may be thinking that you are
being asked to change so very many beliefs. They
may all seem so weird and out of the norm. You
may be thinking, "Nobody I know thinks like this!"

I get it. I have had to consider the fact that,
if this book reaches much of an audience, many
people are going to hate it. They are going to revile
me. Some people take to new ideas like they would
take a broom to a mouse. Some therapist types are
going to hate it because of its lack of orthodoxy.
Medical insurance companies, who grudgingly pay
for treatment that merely reduces psychological
symptoms, will hate anything that promotes the
idea of personal transformation. No doubt, the
quality of the writing will offend some sensibilities.
So be it. I am ready. I truly think this is going to

help some people. Compared to that, who cares about the subjective opinions of others?

Humans have always been tribal, clannish. There is so much comfort to be had in the company of like-minded people. If people do not have a natural clan, they will make them. People who want to believe that marihuana is good for you, or that internet piracy is righteous, or that a mother should breast-feed until the child is four, or that the moon landing was a hoax, or - almost anything - will keep company with people who agree with them. Yahoo! feeds off this with an algorithm in its website that allows it to only bring us news that is like what we have already looked at. One of the most difficult times a patient has in psychotherapy is when they are tempted to adopt a belief that lies outside the bounds of their clan.

I once read that during World War II the United States had its lowest rates of mental illness. It made sense to me. We have maybe never lived in more authentically black-and-white times. Everyone felt they knew who the good guys were. Everyone felt they knew who the bad guys were (and they seemed so very good at being bad!) Everyone knew what their duty was. There was little ambiguity. There was very little call for uncertainty. Everybody had a common "clan" identity.

Our times are so very different.

Uncertainty can be so very distressing. When we are affiliated with a group of like-minded people we feel comforted. It is a state that I can empathize with intellectually, but, obviously, I don't share the same need. I don't have a clan. Perhaps only the clan-less could ever discover that there are better ways of dealing with uncertainty. It takes strength and courage to wander beyond the boundaries of the clan. It takes strength and courage to wander beyond the invisible dog fence of shame. Fortunately, we do tend to value such traits. Most of us would like to think that, if we lived in the American South of 1850, we would have the courage to believe that slavery was wrong. While it may be tempting, it doesn't make sense to put our finger to the wind to judge what is true. We could want our sense of truth and reality to be based on something much more substantial than popular opinion. It has been my hope that evidence and the best available logical argument would be the appealing alternative.

You probably are very brave and have an active, inquisitive mind or you would not have read so far. The benefits of enlightenment are at your doorstep.

It only requires that you recognize that humans have instincts. Everything else is just logic that spools of that like a continuous sheet of aluminum foil. I have no expectation that you just swallow these ideas whole. Give them a test drive.

See if they are not a better explanation for what you see. I did not write this to proselytize. I don't want to start a new clan. I just hope to make a little splash in the great pool of competing ideas and trust to natural selection.

The natural selection of ideas, unfortunately, relies on more than the fitness of the idea. It does take a lot of courage. There is an old movie that demonstrates this well. If you haven't seen it, I'm sure you have seen something similar. In "Twelve Angry Men" Henry Fonda plays a juror who, alone, is convinced of a defendant's innocence. He has the most rational case to be made on the subject, but it flies in the face of the beliefs of the other 11 jurors. No one else but Henry could have stood his ground against the peer pressure of the others. Eventually, Henry wins over another juror – the second bravest; the one who, at the very least, needs the company of one other to keep his insecurity under control. And then there is another… and another. As the jurors come over, the peer pressure shifts until the last holdout cannot stand by his belief any more.

Nobody needs to know what you believe. I know that some of you are extroverts and that your connections to people are so very important to you. We want to be wise in our actions, including deciding who to trust with our confidences. You can be very careful about choosing a Henry Fonda moment. If you are worried about the reaction of the clan, I wouldn't recommend that you trot out these ideas at a dinner party. I've tried it a few times and generally I wind up disappointed. What you will very likely receive is people fighting tooth and claw to defend assumptions they had never considered to be testable. Either that, or they will laugh it off as obviously absurd. It will be as though you are in a Victorian age gentleman's club and just suggested that women should be given the right to vote. When you see that, you know it can't be logic that is driving the argument.

On the other hand, it *is* true that, as you assimilate these ideas, you will care less and less about the opinions of others. You will lose the temptation to think that you can learn something about your value from the subjective opinions of others. More and more, you will hear critical judgements with compassion for what they reveal about the judge and how they must suffer. Your new, *humble* self-esteem will be indestructible.

Early on it will take courage. Maybe this was what the Buddha was thinking when he said that the person wishing for enlightenment needed the motivation of the man running toward a lake with his hair on fire. But, with enlightenment - with the humble self-esteem - courage is less and less necessary. Perhaps this is what Jesus meant when he said that the meek will inherit the earth.

2. Feeling.

Remember the patient who said that she knew that shame was real, because she "felt" it? Feeling can *feel* like truth. I know people who think that anger is bad, because it feels bad. The same can be said about many impulses. We have had frightening experiences in our childhoods that lead to an automatic visceral reaction when we experience certain emotions or impulses. This is the ongoing action of the invisible dog fence.

Just like with other beliefs, we can have beliefs about feelings that lead to automatic maladaptive behavior choices. If we take the feeling about anger *seriously*, we will automatically avoid anger behaviors that would serve our interests. We need to identify and attack these beliefs, just like the others we have been discussing.

We have been doing this already. Anger, for example, might feel bad, but does that really mean that it is? The question becomes: what are we going to believe; our gut, or a rational argument?

What people want, as a part of change, is for the feeling to go away. The process we have been discussing will accomplish this. By merely asking the question, "What are we going to believe?" we have introduced the activity of our frontal lobes (the home of rational thought). By continuing to contemplate the question; by considering the evidence; and by considering the rational argument for a new belief – we strengthen new connections in the wiring of our brain. As these connections with the frontal lobes strengthen, the connections that bring the uncomfortable feeling will recede. Until then, we can begin to think of the feeling as the equivalent of phantom limb pain.

3. Pride.

The proud person doesn't want to change their mind because they feel like their proud belief is the only thing propping them up. They try to use pride as their defense against shame.

I recently saw an overweight, unkempt fellow wearing a dirty T-shirt that read, "I'd rather be sleeping." I have seen many people in the media spotlight who feel that the way to fight back against fat-shaming is to proclaim great pride in their appearance. We all know of people, wounded by the shaming of their families and by social cliques for failures to conform, who will disfigure themselves with tattoos or gauges or extremities of hair or clothes – all to force us to make a judgement about their acceptability to us as quickly as possible.

It is all bravado. It is submission to the black-and-white thinking of the 5-year-old. We cannot eliminate the pernicious effects that shame has on us by clinging to an opposite position. The proud person does not disavow shame, only the shame that applies to the one quality where they feel the most vulnerable to it. It is just about the flimsiest defense against shame imaginable.

Indeed, it strengthens the shamers by making the situation more polarized.

Two children have an argument. It always boils down to:

"Yes, you did."

"No, I didn't."

"Yes, YOU DID!"

"NO, I DIDN'T!"

There is never a winner. Come to think of it, this is what passes for political discourse these days. What we want to do is to eliminate shame, all shame, from our consciousness about the nature of reality; because it is an invalid construct and because it is the plainly logical thing to do.

They say that pride goeth before the fall. This is because of the false certainty that must accompany it. Also, an insistence on a proud position may well blind us to its practical disadvantages to us. It is not shameful to be overweight (much more on this coming up), but it might serve our interests to be more mindful of our health.

4. Victim.

I once had a patient who came to me believing that she had an intractable depression. She had been in psychotherapy for years and had tried numerous medications. She still felt very "depressed". I can be very intrigued by a challenge and, in this case, I jumped in with both feet. I tried new meds. I tried my psychotherapy thing. I didn't make any progress.

One day, it occurred to me that I had been operating with an inaccurate understanding of my patient. She wasn't depressed; she was bitter.

This is how I conceptualized the situation: imagine that you go to a casino and play roulette. Imagine that you bet on black 20 times in a row (nearly a 50-50 bet) and it comes up red 20 times in a row.

There are two ways that you can react to this. You *could* say to yourself that you have just been the recipient of very bad luck. Very bad luck, like very good luck (like winning the lottery) does happen. It is rare, but it does happen. You will conclude that, tomorrow, your luck will be the same as anyone else's.

Or... you *could* say that you were robbed. The perfection instinct will push in this direction. It's just not fair to have such bad luck! And so, a chip forms on your shoulder. You decide that you will not be satisfied, your anger will not be slaked, until you have "won" twenty times in a row.

You won't notice when you have won five times in a row. You will notice the loss on the sixth. You have been denied your due again. Now, there is more anger. Now, you will not be satisfied until you win 21 times in a row. You seem depressed because your eye is always on the negative outcome. With each disappointment, another number is added to the count, like another link on an ever-lengthening chain. I knew a man whose bitterness became so all-encompassing that he cursed God every time he was stopped at an intersection by a red light.

This state of mind makes change impossible. Change brings uncertainty. Change is difficult. Change feels like more bad luck. It feels outrageous to be asked to accept more bad luck before the arrival of the seemingly deserved compensatory good luck.

The problem is – the compensatory good luck is *never* coming. The odds are like winning the lottery twice, in a row. With my patient, and others like her, my approach turned to helping her grieve the fact that she had been the recipient of very bad luck and her compensation was never coming. With grieving, the fact of the matter can be accepted and the patient can start fresh. With this patient, the approach worked with remarkable speed. Her "depression" was cured.

Bitterness can lead to the belief that one has been a victim. This is another difficult trap. There is much that reinforces the victim stance. It is a black-and-white position that relives the believer of uncertainty. The victim is always in the right. Disagreement must always be wrong and someone else will always be found to serve as a useful scapegoat. The victim is spared from the risky proposition of having to look inward and perhaps see something that feels shameful. All of the shame is projected outward. I find people who want to see themselves as victims to be some of the most difficult people to help in psychotherapy.

Victims can form a clan. Now we have a perfect storm opposing change. A patient once told me that affiliation with a victim clan is like being in a crab trap. I didn't know it at the time, but apparently, the only thing that keeps a crab in a crab trap is the other crabs. When one tries to escape, the other crabs grab it and pull it back in. When my patient tried to change, she was assaulted by a barrage of shaming from her victim clan of origin. They were desperate to keep the comforting fabric of the group-think entirely intact.

I am not denying that victimization occurs (I can imagine the anger rising in some of you). Some people are more powerful than others and will sometimes use that power differential to take advantage of the weak. It's just that bitterness and victimhood offer no chance for healing. The black-and-white perspective must always be an oversimplification. Victimization does not need to lead to *identity*.

It's very hard to get a victimizer (and their supporters) to change when they are being assigned 100% of the blame (and, of course, it's always a shaming blame). It is then much more likely that *their* sense of things being unfair will be aroused. The situation just becomes more polarized. Shame makes it impossible to create the objective narrative that can lead to understanding, compassion and healing.

5. Winning.

Come to think of it, perhaps it is the polarization of our times that digs our heels in the most. It can feel as though, if we give an inch, it will be snapped up by a tireless enemy. We might feel that the best defense is to augment our beliefs. Change them?! Bah!!

To tell the truth, when I first considered the need to address this form of resistance, I felt a bit daunted. But then, I considered how much mediation between polarized camps is part of what I do all the time. And as we will find, everything we have been going over already leads to the path out of this quagmire.

First of all, polarization cannot exist but for black-and-white thinking. Resolution requires that there be a third path that is acceptable to both parties. What would that look like?

If you find that changing beliefs seems dangerous, try this thought exercise: Watch a television program that captures the essence your opposition. Get a piece of paper and score each sentence for the following:

1. Motivated by the perfection instinct.

2. Is an example of black-and-white thinking.

3. Involves notions of shame.

4. Preys on feelings of insecurity.

5. Embodies maladaptive self-esteem management strategies.

You will be hardly surprised when the transcript gets a very high score! The second part is a little more difficult: do the same thing for a show from your side. I'm betting that the scores will be similar!

Now we can see our way clear to the third path. Neither side is engaged in anything you have been reading about thus far. What we are considering is like a different plane of existence. Indeed, anyone who integrates the ideas I've been suggesting may have to wait a very long time before they have an opportunity to "vote their conscience." In the meantime, we can vote in accordance with our interests and believe what we want.

It may feel like we must be immovable if we are to protect the things we value. It just may be, however, that we could value enlightenment above all else.

6. Wrong.

Maybe you have been trapped in a reality battle. Maybe your parents told you that your feelings were invalid or mislabeled them for you. You may feel like I am trying to do the same – but I am not. I am 100% in favor of your feelings. I am sure that they make sense. All I am suggesting is that you consider *your* interests. I am on *your* side. Declare your victory!

I once saw a fellow whose first words to me were that he didn't want to see me. His wife had issued an ultimatum, so he came. He believed that any reliance upon anybody or anything was a sign of utter shame. He had no trouble acknowledging his suffering, but his belief that shear willpower would lead him to overcome it was unshakable.

The man was an attorney. Such was his need to be right, that he made a living from it. Sadly, in one important instance, he was dead wrong.

He is an example of the common notion of the neurotic; the one who tries the same thing over and over – expecting a different outcome. Such is the power of some beliefs.

It can be very hard to be wrong. We can put a tremendous amount of time and energy into a belief. Change would mean that we acknowledge and accept that it was all for nothing. This is what Jesus was getting at when he said that it would be easier for a camel to pass through the eye of a needle than for a rich man to enter heaven. It's not the riches. It's the effort that went into getting them. Perhaps, it is also the sense of superiority the rich man attaches to his wealth. And now, he must accept that it is for naught? That he has been wrong; when all the signals were telling him that he was right?

This could be happening right now, to you. What I have written may be feeling like an affront to beliefs you hold dear. If so, you have my sympathy. The only solace I can offer is that you need not change all at once. You can let the new beliefs percolate. If you are brave enough, you can collect more data. You can give yourself the time you need to grieve your losses. And perhaps, at the very least, you can disentangle yourself from the idea that it is *shameful to be wrong*.

People who need to be right can also form a clan. It is another perfect storm opposing change. Such clans are the ultimate example of the self-affirming echo chamber. Their need for certainty is absolute. Tyrants have often taken advantage of such groups by co-opting their conformity. You might think that members of such groups would be the least interested in enlightenment, but I have discovered delightful exceptions over the years.

7. Difficult.

It can seem like it should be easy to change a belief. I can have a belief about the relative safety of a medication. I can read a high quality piece of research and, poof, my belief is shifted. With what we have been reviewing, it can be much harder to change a belief.

This can be true even when we are motivated to change. Often, feelings and visceral reactions get in the way. They may suggest to us that the present belief is true. They may suggest to us that the new belief is too scary to be true. The hoarder can feel such horror at the prospect of throwing something away. The shy person can feel such horror at the prospect of asking someone out. The abused wife can feel such horror at the prospect of being alone.

We are often confronted by a wish for change that is difficult to realize. I remember my daughter becoming so frustrated by the pace of her developing soccer skills. I would always calmly reassure her that the practice was working. I would tell her that, as she was sleeping, her brain would be saying, "It seems we have a new and very important priority here. How can we divert resources and streamline processes to deliver what the master wants?" This is, in effect, exactly what the brain does.

I would tell my daughter that, tomorrow, she would notice a little bit of improvement. Fortunately, this prediction came true more often than not!

This is exactly what will happen when you "practice" the processes that promote changes of belief. The brain will deliver what you want by tuning up the contribution of the frontal lobes and tuning down emotional and visceral contributions.

We have character "suspects" that also can make change difficult. Common ones include "not smart enough" or "not quick enough." One day, in my own psychotherapy, I caught myself musing upon the idea that, somewhere, at the same moment, there was another psychotherapy patient who was just like me – only doing better!

Every pilgrimage is unique because every pilgrim and every starting place is unique. If there can never be more than one particular car on our particular racetrack, it makes no sense to think we are going fast or slow. There is never any comparison to make.

It's hard to wait for change. Shame fuels this. Time and again, I will see patients try to force a change in behavior on themselves. They can't wait to prove that they are no longer "defective." It is always a white knuckling affair that cannot be sustained. I must gently bring them back to the view that, if they change their beliefs, the behaviors will take care of themselves.

Change is difficult and it is uncomfortable. We will often lapse back into old habits - even if they harm us - because of the comfort of the familiar. We have to try very hard not to see this as shameful failure. It is the norm. Change often comes like the stock market. There will be short term ups and downs, but it is the long term trend that matters.

Some will protect themselves from the discomfort of change by telling themselves that change is impossible. We can call this the "hopelessness defense". It is different from the pessimism that comes with depression, because it is especially applied to the change process. If a problem can be identified as impossible, then the one with the problem can be let off the hook. Of course, the "hook" is all about shame. Once we can see our state in objective terms, there is *no reason to think of it as hopeless.*

8. Forever.

I once had a very anxious patient who had great difficulty changing. His body told him that any venture beyond his usual comfort zone was dangerous. Over time, his comfort zone was constricting in upon him, like a python. It was easy to find the elements from his past that made him vulnerable to uncertainty. It was easy to identify the difference between likely risks and those he felt. When he came to therapy it was often clear that he hadn't even retained much of what we had been doing to shift his beliefs.

One day, it became clear to me that the problem was that he felt that change was *forever.* He was going to have the same discomfort forever. The benefits of change were theoretical, but the pain was real.

In this case we had to work towards a "day at a time" approach. I suggested that he only needed to take the beliefs out on a test drive. It was just fine to be a very picky car buyer. He could take as many test drives as he wanted.

We don't need to make a commitment to the change, just to the test drive. If the new belief is true, the tests will bring us evidence of this. This is what Jesus meant when he said, "Act as if you have faith, and faith will be given you."

***

Friedrich Nietzsche once said, "The snake which cannot cast his skin has to die. As well the minds which are prevented from changing their opinions; they cease to be mind."

Fat

*You know what happens when you get shamed
for your unhealthy body image? Well if you're
semi-intellegent (sic)(ironic), you'll make some
healthy changes. Goodbye fat. Goodbye shame.
Hello health and real body pride. You want to
love your body? Then have a lovable one.*
An internet blogger best kept anonymous

In the bizarre world of shame the front lines
of battle are all about fat. Fat shamers and anti-fat
shamers are constantly launching salvos at each
other. The fat shamers seem determined to shame.
What is it about fat?

The fat shamers won't want to accept this,
but it is all about their plan for managing self-
esteem. They are thin (or fit, or buff, or whatever)
and they want to feel superior to others because of
it. They would have great difficulty accepting that
their fitness is a matter of luck or that fatness is as
well.

It is luck, however. It is the luck of their
chromosomes. It is the luck of their upbringing.
Circumstances conspired so that they could
develop the self-discipline they possess.
Circumstances conspired so that they came to think
of thinness as something superior to begin with.
They were unlucky enough that they didn't
develop a healthier self-esteem strategy.

Truth be told, I'm not even sure it is truly self-discipline. Self-discipline is conventionally thought of as involving doing something difficult without immediate gratification. However, take the thin-proud person away from their food preoccupations, their hours in the gym, their runs, with babies in tow in expensive strollers, and they will feel immediate *distress*. Stopping is the hard thing. They run the risk of gaining a pound, losing some tone or an increment of stamina. This is the true measure of how much self-esteem is wrapped up in this.

For the sake of *health*, we need about 30 minutes of moderate aerobic exercise a day. Everything above this is for the sake of something else. And, it could be noted, it comes at the expense of *everything* else. The opportunity costs include care of children, improvement of relationships, improvement of the community, acquisition of knowledge... etc. People are certainly entitled to their preferences, but such preferences do not make one superior to another.

What fat shamers also do not want to accept is that fat is all luck too. Let's begin with chromosomes. Humans have adapted to the environments they live in. People from very hot climates acquired long, thin frames to facilitate heat dissipation. People from cold climates acquired short, thick frames for the opposite reason. People from high altitudes acquired the ability to use oxygen more efficiently.

One problem that has hounded mankind for most of its history has been famine. What would we want to acquire to combat this? It would be the ability to conserve energy stores when food is scarce and to add energy stores rapidly when food is plenty. Adult onset diabetes (Type II) is the ultimate example of this. With this form of diabetes, the body loses some of it sensitivity to the effects of insulin. Insulin is the hormone that drives sugar from the bloodstream into the tissues. The body responds to this by making more insulin. Higher than normal blood levels of insulin make us crave carbohydrates. The more we eat, the hungrier we get.

This is one of the reasons why diets *never* work. A diet creates an artificial famine. The body goes to work conserving calories. Dieters know this as the dreaded plateau. One finds that they are not losing weight despite consuming considerably fewer calories than they are used to. They find that they are hungry all the time. They become discouraged and give up. They eat as they did before, but now, they no longer experience satiety. In almost no time, one weighs a little more than they did before.

Eating is not optional. In parts of the world where obesity is epidemic, famine is no longer a threat. A body that worked well for 99% of human history now doesn't work so well. And we add shame insult to the injury. Black skin evolved from a need to protect bodies from the sun. Now that we have sun screen, surely we don't have reason to shame blackness?

The Pima Indians of the American Southwest have been scientifically established as the world's most obese people. In other words, (perhaps not surprising, given the climate where they live) they are the best prepared for famine. Among them, even adolescents have a high rate of adult onset diabetes. The U.S. government has spent truckloads of money trying to learn how to make a fat Pima thin. They still don't know.

Across the border, in Mexico, there are Pima Indians who are as skinny as rails. They are genetically identical to their U.S. cousins. What is their secret? They work all week in the fields at hard physical labor and they eat rice... and beans. They didn't volunteer for this.

Those most likely to spend incredible amounts of time maintaining their bodies and shaming fat people for being inferior may quickly say, "Yeah, rice and beans. Work out. I could do that. Fat Pimas should be ashamed of themselves." But they will not have taken their many other advantages into account.

Fat people are often raised by fat people. People without self-discipline are often raised by people without self-discipline. People with poor knowledge of healthy eating habits are often raised by people without knowledge of healthy eating habits. And many of us, fat shamers included, have our beliefs seared into our minds long before we can think abstractly.

My daughter has been, in some ways, luckier than me. She was born with hip dysplasia, but it was caught early, when it was easily treatable (otherwise exercise would become misery). She has always been provided with healthy foods to choose from. They were food choices that, because of expense, would not be available to many. She had a natural passion for sports. She had a father who was willing to spend hundreds of hours with her; not just helping to polish technique, but teaching her mastery over the painful elements of training. Sports are expensive and therefore not available to many. She has a touch of asthma, but this has not held her back because of the medical care we provided for her (at an expense not manageable by many). She has inherited some of my glucose intolerance, but found out early and has had to make little change to a diet that comes naturally to her. As a young adult, playing sports and being physically active come naturally to her. Without just one of these elements, she would very likely be overweight.

Fat shamers do not pause to consider the tremendous luck and the tremendous privilege that made it possible for them to feel superior. It would be much more seemly if they could merely felt gratitude.

And it is a sort of privilege that must be present from the beginning. Poor Oprah Winfrey seems to have plenty of privilege these days. But she has scars from early in life and a resulting relationship with shame that have given her an emptiness that no amount of food or money or fame or power can ever fill.

There was a whole generation of us scarred by the Great Depression. For many, starvation was a genuine prospect. Having too little to eat was considered shameful and wasting food was the ultimate sin. Eating indulgently was a wonderful treat.

All of this set up the worst beliefs about food at just the time in history when cheap, delicious food was to become perpetually, easily available.

I sure wish that I was never encouraged to "clean my plate". I wish I hadn't been taught that there were certain foods that were an amazing treat and then not taught how to enjoy *not* eating them. I wish that I wasn't taught that the worst thing about Thanksgiving was the limit of our stomach's capacity.

Shame makes people more likely to be obese. There is abundant research that shows this to be true. It makes sense too. If we have a low sense of worthiness we are not going to be good at wanting/getting things. We are very likely to be feeling deprived and empty. Food is an indulgence that can happen quickly and on the sly. With it, we don't have to worry about stepping on anybody's toes.

Behaviors that promote a healthy weight will almost always come at somebody else's expense. We must feel *very* worthy (but not necessarily superior) to pull them off. Running, to the extent that anyone is depending on us, will take something away from them. No matter how much is spent on that fancy stroller, the baby would probably rather be doing something else. The vegan will always make party planning or restaurant picking more difficult than it otherwise would have been. This is not a bad thing (I can never do black-and-white). Selfishness is a thing we want to be wise about and attention to *health* can be pretty wise.

I have been a thin person and I have been a fat person. As a child, I was called "husky". Looking back at the pictures, I can realize that, at the very same time I was being taught terrible eating habits, I was being given a shameful body image very much out of proportion to my true shape. In college, I played tennis all the time and could comfortably fit into extra small shorts when I played. 10 years ago, I began flirting with size 2X. At my last appointment with my doctor I got to hear those precious words, "You don't have to lose any more weight."

Along the way I was exposed to a lot of the elements that make it hard to be thin. Many were contributed by the diet industry. I succumbed to their charlatan tactics more than once. I tried the outfit that emphasizes "watching". During the week, I would watch what I ate. Every week I had to go to a meeting. Before every meeting I would be weighed. If I had lost weight, there would be smiles and cheers. If I had held even or gained, there would be sad faces and vacuous solace. The scale dictated everything. There was no consideration of what I had *done* during the last week. I could have lost weight because I had put my finger down my throat after every meal. I could have gained weight despite following the diet to the letter. The feedback would still have depended solely upon the verdict of the scale.

I tried the diet where you are given prepackaged food. I was especially motivated at the time because I was in the last year of my residency/psychotherapy and I (mistakenly) believed that being thin was verification that I was ready to move on. I lost about 30 pounds and got to my goal weight. I was hungry and cold all the time. I found myself yearning for the promised "maintenance diet"- thus far kept secret from me - in the hope that I could eat more and be hungry less. Imagine my disappointment when the maintenance diet was revealed and allowed for the same number of calories per day that I had already been consuming.

Another reason all diets *must* fail is that they require changes in behavior that are too extreme to be sustainable. Especially when we are not good at wanting/getting, the sense of deprivation and hardship is too great. And remember how poorly shame effects reinforcement. When every pound lost is nothing more than diminished shame, all we are getting for our suffering is a little less kicking.

I yo-yo dieted my way up to the precipice of 2X. Along the way I developed adult onset diabetes. I am not naturally a litigious person, but someone should go after the diet industry in the way they went after the tobacco industry. It is an industry that is killing people. They know it. They don't care.

My doctor knew about my weight gain. I complained to her about being tired all the time as well as gaining weight. She was known for being compulsive with her tests, but she failed to order the test I needed. She was a naturally thin person who prioritized her exercise time above just about everything else. She asked me about my exercise. She laughed at my answer.

It's a sort of dirty secret in the medicine business that they do a terrible job teaching doctors how to say, "I'm sorry, it is not within my ability to help this problem." Therefore, one of their favorite go-to strategies, when faced with this awful flirtation with humility, is to blame the patient. Every day, millions of patients are told to lose weight by doctors who have no idea how such a feat might be accomplished.

The self-esteem strategy of feeling superior appears, on the surface, to have some advantages. It certainly imparts a robust sense of entitlement which, in turn, facilitates engagement in the behaviors that make a feeling of superiority possible. But the cost is significant. It is a fragile self-esteem that is enslaved by its criterion for superiority (be it intelligence, competence, or six-pack abs). It requires constant maintenance at the expense of everything else. It represents a self-delusion that leads to failures of judgement (think Lance Armstrong). It precludes personal growth. It precludes the capacity for compassion. It undermines the fabric of society.

It is superiority that enables feelings of contempt. It is much more effective than familiarity. Research has shown that contempt is the number one killer of relationships.

A patient of mine once told a story about a "friend" of hers. The patient had benefitted greatly from her psychotherapy. The friend had problems very like those the patient had overcome. The friend had a "must be superior" self-esteem strategy. In this case, the criterion for superiority was intelligence and the proof was a PhD. The friend adamantly denied that it was possible that anybody could ever benefit from psychotherapy ("and certainly not me"). To think otherwise would be too humbling. It would represent a crack in the superiority armor. The friend went on to weaken the bonds of friendship by belittling my patient's experience by saying, "It's well known that people get wiser as they age."

Well, maybe some of us.

My friend, the Ivy League trained lawyer, once had an opportunity to have dinner with a Supreme Court Justice. He was joined by several classmates enslaved by the need for superiority. They may well have wasted many of the opportunities presented by the occasion by trying to one-up each other with the pithiness and impressiveness of the legal questions they asked the Justice. My friend may have fared much better when he was rewarded with a half hour conversation following the question, "So, how are the kids?"

10 years ago, I was diagnosed with a sleep disorder. The effect of treatment was like putting on glasses for the first time. I and my perception of the world were instantly transformed. I woke up and I felt like exercising! Since then I've put over 7,000 miles on my treadmill. I work out 90% of my days. I have gone on cruises and come home weighing less than before I left. The reason for my weight gain and my habits had always been best understood in objective terms (rather than

166

subjective/shaming terms). The degree of complexity applicable to such an understanding could be great but, in one critical way, it was very simple. But more than anything, it was all luck.

There are two proven ways to lose weight if you are obese (and don't have a secondary condition responsible for it). The first is bariatric surgery (your GI tract is altered so that you cannot eat very much and absorb so many calories). The second is to devote your entire life to weight loss; including how you are going to make your living (think – Subway Jared). There may be a steep price to pay if you devote so much time to weight loss and not to other important issues in your life (think – Subway Jared).

There may be a third way. I can't prove it to you. For another way to work it would have to overcome the two big obstacles to weight loss: the body's defense against famine and the need to assimilate habits that are markedly different from what we are used to. It *must* involve habits. Establishing and keeping a healthy weight must involve the maintenance of certain habits… for a *lifetime.*

There is only one way we could possibly fool the body's defenses and assimilate a lot of unfamiliar and potentially uncomfortable habits: gradually and incrementally. Most of us don't mind brushing our teeth and do it every day. We need to take on the habits of healthy weight maintenance in steps no more painful than tooth brushing. Here is the outline of what such a plan would look like:

Rule #1. Throw the scale away. It is the enemy. It is the tool of the shame devil (if such an entity were to exist).

Rule #2. Be gradual. Gradual is the next best thing to painless. The first habit to adopt is the habit of writing down what you eat. Don't even start with a goal of doing it every day. Be pleased with yourself if it can be most days out of a week. Don't worry about restricting what you eat. Remember, our *total focus* is on habit acquisition.

Rule #3. Be liberal with positive reinforcement (rewards). Just don't let them be caloric rewards. A diet Mountain Dew works wonders for me (but only one per day for me). I only get one if I get up at my desired, but difficult, time (4:45 AM). This gives me plenty of time to work out before work.

I take an online Spanish class that employs "game theory." They give rewards - "Lingots" - for all kinds of accomplishments. I must tell you, a lingot must be just about the most worthless thing on the planet and yet, they make a difference. You could give yourself dollars – guilt free "HabitBucks." You can buy some very cool stuff with them!

Rule #4. Habit progression. The idea is to ratchet things up slowly enough and, therefore, painlessly enough. This will also help biologically, because your body may be fooled into thinking that there is no famine happening. I know the temptation to be impatient. Such impatience is driven by shame and the easy-fix, diet industry bandits. The habits we are aiming for are life-long. You have plenty of time. Think of special rewards you might give yourself for sticking with the new habit goal for a week, a month, three months, and a year. In the Spanish course, I am rewarded for every 10 consecutive days of practice. You can get hooked on keeping a streak alive (I'm up to 1100 days!).

Here is what the progression could look like. Each step can take weeks. I don't know the right number for you. I trust your judgement. Just don't stop. If you feel uncomfortable with the progression, then slow down or back up a step. And don't stop being impressed with your progress (no matter what the shame trolls you bump into might say). Don't move to the next step until the step you are on is no more painful than brushing your teeth.

Goal 1. Write down everything you eat, at least most of the days in a week, for several weeks. You don't need to put any effort into food restriction. It would be better if you didn't (but this can be difficult when you are being accountable to yourself like this).

Goal 2. Write down everything you eat, *every* day, for several weeks (I'll stop repeating the "several weeks" part now).

Goal 3. Write everything down and, more often than not, include the calories in each item or serving. I still don't care if you put any effort into food restriction. This step is plenty hard enough. It will involve some inconvenience and ingenuity. You should start thinking about a special reward for completing the next step.

Goal 4. Write down everything, calories and all, for a month straight.

At this point you may have noticed some weight loss. I know – no scale – but, still, you may have noticed. Some people just can't help but lose weight when they are being accountable to themselves. Congratulations then! You may be on your way. But be on the alert for the possibility that you are asking too much of yourself just now. If so, give yourself more time. On the other hand, if you are feeling strong and weight loss is not evident...

Goal 5. Calculate the average number of calories consumed per day over the last two weeks. Now shoot for 5% less, more days than not.

I'm sure you get the drill from here out. From most days to every day. From 5% every day to 10% most days, and so on – until there is evidence of a change. When there is evidence, hold fast. Resist the temptation to rush things and continue the progression. If you don't, your body might take notice and fight you. Take pleasure in fooling your body. Remember, we want this to be as painless as possible. If things seemed stalled for a month or two, then consider another progression.

You can do something similar with exercise. I emphasized eating habits first because it is almost impossible to lose weight with exercise alone. As with eating habits, try to be very mindful of opportunities for positive reinforcement. Think of all the advantages of being lighter, stronger, more agile and having increased stamina. We can never buy youth (what the plastic surgeons sell is the illusion of youth), but if we can be in better shape than we were 5 years ago, it's the next best thing. It's best to consider the advantages of weight loss in terms of what we might *do* rather than how we might *appear*. Focus on appearance tends to lead us too close to the tar pit of shame.

Start easy. If you join a club that has one, just go and sit in the hot tub for 15 minutes (if you are into that sort of thing). Remember, our focus is always on the development of habits. If you prefer to exercise at a club, it is essential to develop the habit of *going to the club*. We need to make the exercise habits as close to painless and automatic (like brushing teeth) as possible. As with eating habits, think of rewards you can give yourself for reaching exercise habit goals.

Gradually work up to more frequency, time and intensity. Habits are going to feel more "habitual" if not doing them feels very exceptional. As I write this, I am in my 50's. I work out almost every day; an hour on weekdays; more on the weekends.

What I have found is that, once I noticed the benefits of the habits, I didn't want to lose them – and that this helps preserve the habits.

In addition to your focus on positive reinforcement, work to reduce negative reinforcement. Do everything you can think of to make exercise as palatable as possible. I prefer to work out at home (convenience, privacy, control of environment). You may like a gym. Especially at first, pick the form of exercise that you like to do the most, if you can do it reliably.

Seek to diminish what you don't like about exercise. For me it is boredom and sweating. I make sure plenty of fans are around to make me comfortable. I'm big into audiovisual entertainment distractions. The TV is always on the channel of my choosing; but that is not enough - I go for multi-media. I love to read the New Yorker. The only place I allow myself to read it is on my treadmill!

Later, if you have a menu of things you do when working out, do the things you like the least, first (for me, it is ab-work). Then the things you like best will feel like a reward too.

For me, there is an ultimate reward. On weekends and when I'm on vacation, you will probably find me walking in the wilderness!

Addiction

*If I were in control I'd have the police round up
all the hard addicts and put them into camps.
They would be forced to work, therefore
contributing to society, as opposed to sitting in a
piss scented alley shooting up and nodding out
all day. If they refuse to work, they would be
swiftly executed.*
Anonymous Internet Troll

Wow. I knew I had to start with that
quote as soon as I saw it. I had been planning to
use one from Carl Jung - mostly because I was
amused by how it revealed him to be a black-and-
white thinker (at least once) - but this was
perfect. My father had a passion for his own "if I
was in charge" monologues. Apparently, there
are an amazing number of complex problems that
would be easily solved if we had the right people
in charge! Do you need any more evidence for a
perfection (importance+potency) instinct?

This poor internet troll. No doubt he has
had a great deal of misfortune in his life. He is
bitter and he is suffering. He can't help himself.
But he speaks for a significant number of us who
think of addiction as something shameful.
Addiction can seem like a particularly sinister
member in our lineup of reasons to have doubts
about our worthiness.

I saw a patient with addiction problems the other day. It was our second visit together. At the first visit, I had made some suggestions to him. When I saw him back for the second time, I couldn't help but notice that he was fighting back tears. It turned out that he had done some of what I had suggested, but not all. He hadn't been perfect and he was sure he was about to catch shame-hell from me. I told him that I was impressed by the progress he had made. I told him my bit about reinforcement strategies and perfection expectations. In time, he was fighting back tears for a completely different reason. I know I am the only person he had ever met who reacted to his difficulties in such a way.

I wasn't always so sanguine with such matters. My mother's addictions created hard feelings in me. My training included learning about addiction. This included a spell in an inpatient chemical dependency treatment facility. Before graduating from the facility, each patient was required to present their plan for recovery, and all of us – staff and patients – had to give feedback. One day, I heard a plan that was absurdly doomed to fail. I then heard all of the patients give nothing but praise to the plan. I shamed them all. I suspect I was eloquent. Afterward, one of the staff came up to me and shamed me viciously for what I had said. Sigh.

Addicts can challenge our capacity for compassion. They do things that hurt us a lot. It seems like they are making terrible choices that we would never make. If free will existed, we would have every reason to think poorly of them.

For addiction to not be shameful it must be, as in all things, that there is a rational, objective explanation for the behavior of the addict. It must be that they are doing the best they can... under the circumstances. Fortunately, this is true.

Let's once again start with biology. Drugs that are addictive can have very pleasant effects on us. Once, I had a big dose of an opiate before a procedure for kidney stones and have never experienced such a comforting sense of peacefulness.

I said that they *can* have pleasant effects. In part this is because the sensation of "pleasantness" is genetically mediated. Whenever my father got a big dose of opiate he would only become delirious and combative (unpleasant for all of us). With every drug of abuse, there will be a spectrum of experiences among us from unpleasant, to "meh", to "this is the home I've been waiting for all my life." Where we fall on that spectrum is something completely outside of our control.

Addictive drugs have three different tricks they use to trap us. First, they mimic something our brains do, only more intensely. Opiates do this by attaching to endorphin receptors. Marihuana does this by attaching to endocannabinoid receptors. The systems that use these receptors are meant to operate in a coordinated balance. The brain has machinery that maintains that balance. These drugs wash the system with a tidal wave of excess molecules attaching themselves to receptors in the brain. The brain reacts to this by trying to restore the balance. When the drug leaves the brain, it leaves the brain slightly askew because of the effort to seek balance. If using the drug seemed like a good idea the first time around, now it will seem like a little bit better idea.

It is a siren-song situation. The pleasures of the drug lure us in. We can't detect the brain's efforts to restore a balance. Only after it is too late do we recognize that we have been trapped.

An example of this phenomenon, that helps demonstrate how we are truly trapped, involves nose spay decongestants. They are addictive. I've seen the addicts. It may be hard to imagine that we could ever find ourselves "jonesing" for nose spray, but all the elements of addiction I just described can happen.

Nose spray decongestants flood us with molecules like the ones our bodies use to modulate the "stuffiness" of our noses. The pleasantness they impart is relief from nasal congestion (which can be truly unpleasant). The body goes to work making more receptors for these molecules. After the nose spray has worn off, we are a little more likely to be stuffy than before we used it.

The second trick of addictive drugs is to stimulate the brain to release its own tidal wave of molecular signals. Mostly, this involves the neurotransmitter molecule called dopamine. Dopamine is involved in the "reward system" of the brain. This system is what tells us something was a good idea – like sex or eating something delicious. Especially in our more primitive ancestors, this is an important brain system for navigating in life.

Cocaine, meth and nicotine have this effect (to varying degrees). They become addictive because they ask more of the production system for these molecules than it can deliver. After the drugs are used, the molecules, in effect, go on "back order". If using the drug felt like a good idea at first - now, not using the drug feels like a bad idea. In time, the machinery backlog becomes so great that it's hard to get the reward. We simply are trying to avoid the discomfort that comes from not using.

The third trick is to throw off the system that regulates "alertness". We can think of the brain as having a "gas pedal." It is what makes us alert and it runs on a molecular signal called glutamate. We also have a "brake pedal" that runs on a signal called GABA. The reason we have this coordinated system is because, if you consider man in his natural environment – like out on the savanna – he needs a lot of gas pedal, because there are animals about that want to eat him. Of course, he also needs brake pedal, to be able to relax and have restorative sleep. The system is designed to move back and forth, depending of the needs of the moment. In effect, the left foot knows what the right foot is doing and vice versa.

Alcohol and tranquilizers (like the benzodiazepine medications you may have heard of – Valium, Xanax, Ativan – among many) work on this system. They press down on the brake pedal. If you are anxious, this can feel like a pretty good idea. The problem, once again, is the brain's stubborn pursuit of balance. It recognizes the heavy foot on the brake pedal and goes to work making more glutamate receptors. Now, the gas pedal is touchier than it was before.

There is another way that biology is involved. It has to do with the nature of the adolescent brain. Adolescents tend to be foolish and rash. They tend to think of themselves as invulnerable. It may be that this is important for our species. Once again, consider man in his natural element; the one we have spent the bulk of our time in; the one we were designed for. In this element, we lived in small, widely dispersed bands. Procreation would require either interbreeding or somebody foolish enough to venture across the dangerous territory that separated the bands. Enter the adolescent. He (the male pronoun is perhaps more apt) is perfectly designed for the job! Unfortunately, he is also perfectly designed to fall for the siren song of drugs.

Now let's talk about the psychology of addiction. There is much that works against the possibility of free will. Remember how, early on, I spoke of the fundamental challenges of adult life: frustration, disappointment, discouragement, uncertainty and assaults on our self-esteem. Recall also how it is that we are dependent on models for whatever talents we develop for the management of these problems. If the modelling is maladaptive, it is highly likely that our management skills will be limited. So, if our parents could never handle these things, we run the risk of stumbling into very maladaptive strategies; like turning the problems over to drugs. This is especially likely if our parents model the drug use strategy (which is not at all uncommon).

At first, drugs seem like a good idea. They are very good at taking anger, sadness, doubt and anxiety away. This is another part of the siren song. The problem is that the source of these emotions does not go away. Real coping requires the assimilation of adaptive beliefs. What follows from such an assimilation is an automatic way of acting that sustains us through difficulties.

We know that it takes thousands of hours of practice to be good at something. This holds true for the management of our fundamental challenges. Our skills must be strengthened like a muscle. Every hour spent giving problems over to drugs is an hour lost. Every opportunity lost makes us weaker.

There is another fundamental challenge that is especially prevalent today – boredom. There is a huge industry, continuously at work, delivering the message that boredom is a horrible state to be avoided at all costs. And, of course, for a price, it is now possible to be continuously diverted and entertained at every moment in time.

It is a state of affairs that is making us weaker. Boredom, like necessity, is the mother of invention. A child will come to us and complain of boredom. If we require them to invent something that will address this situation, it is one of the wonderful aspects of the human condition that they *will*.

Belief that boredom is bad steals from our chances for enlightenment. It teams up with shame to keep our minds continuously focused outward. Without shame, one of the most interesting things we might do is quietly consider our thoughts. They will, invariably, bring us solutions to problems; help us plan for the future; bring us pleasant memories or useful feelings; or help us create something interesting. How very tragic it is that we have been acculturated to believe that *our own thoughts* are something to be avoided. How much beauty is missing in our world because of this? How many problems have gone unaddressed?

Drugs can certainly be entertaining. Or they can enhance the experience of being entertained. Once, when I was watching the Northern Lights with a small group, I heard someone say, "I sure wish I could be high for this." I can't say they were wrong. The wish to be entertained certainly is not shameful. But, just as with every other impulse we have reviewed, we want to be wise about how we put the impulse into action. Using drugs as a singular strategy for avoiding boredom cannot be said to be wise.

Unfortunately, the final snap of the siren song trap occurs because it does not dawn on the user just how unwise the chosen coping strategy has been until it is quite late. Years can go by with things seeming to be good enough before the addict begins slipping into the behaviors we find so annoying. Then, the prospect of recovery seems horribly daunting. One must consider the possibility of thousands of hours of catch-up work; all the while experiencing the pains that all the fundamental challenges bring... *full force*.

There is an additional element, which seems like a mixture of biology and psychology, which I think of as the last twist of the knife. It involves a sort of selective memory that is beyond conscious control. The addict finds that it is much easier to remember the very pleasant experiences they had because of drug use than the bad experiences. These memories sing their seductive song to the user all the time.

Shame, of course, makes all of this worse. It helps keep us in denial that we have a problem. It makes it much harder to seek help. It creates the expectation that we will never be received with compassion. It makes it harder to appreciate small victories. And, perhaps most of all, it brings a particular pain from which we could wish for escape.

Shame also often undermines treatment. Remember how it is so very difficult for many of us (not just addicts) to deal with uncertainty. There is a temptation to substitute false certainty – dogma. There are many who will tell us that there is one and only one way to recover from addiction. It's quite remarkable how many different "only one" ways we can bump into. One sad, common element is the labeling of any deviation from the proscribed course as shameful. But seriously, what could be more uncertain than how a unique individual should recover from addiction.

"One way" thinkers focus on action. Very possibly this is because they are uncomfortable looking at their thoughts. It is so much better to focus on beliefs. If we can shift them, the actions will take care of themselves.

Competence

Whatever is worth doing at all is worth doing well.
Philip Stanhope, 4th Earl of Chesterfield

I can't exactly remember if my father said these words. It doesn't matter, because everything he did, seared the sentiment into my bones.

Not long ago, I bought a car with a manual transmission. It had been 25 years since I had driven one. It so happened that, when I showed it to my daughter, she had just bought her first car. It also had a manual transmission.

We were driving my car and I missed a shift. I reflexively grimaced with self-reproach at the mistake. My daughter noticed and, with ironic cheerfulness, said "Dad, you and I are just alike. I would have reacted in the same way!"

Now I had another reason for self-reproach. I had passed the curse to another generation. Then I paused and caught myself. I had no reason to think that I could shift flawlessly. I had no reason to think I could have parented flawlessly. There could be no shame in imperfection. I had done the best I possibly could at every moment in time... under the circumstances.

Over the years (and still some now) the list of activities I have had to catch myself with has been long. Just a small sampling could include:

knot tying; screw driver turning; igloo building; fly casting; diapering; losing even a trivial thing; handwriting; the neatness of my charts; being late; getting lost; trimming a sail; cooking; making anything; pruning (or failure to prune); canoe paddling; writing this damn sentence. If it's worth doing, it's worth doing well.

It just isn't so. The sentiment doesn't serve our interests very well at all. There are tremendous opportunity costs associated with doing something well. Every minute spent upgrading beyond good enough should have to compete with everything else we can do with our time. And it takes exponentially more time to get from the 80th percentile of good to the 90th; and from there to the 95th; and to the 99th and so on.

The way I write my medical notes can serve as an example. A bonafide, grade-A initial exam is supposed to include a "Review of Systems" (basically, a check-list of things the patient *doesn't* have) and a "Mini Mental Status Exam" (a screen for defects in cognition – like memory). While the value of these is arguable; I frequently do not do them because the likelihood that they will add to my understanding is small and it is so much more valuable to spend the time establishing a rapport with my patient and beginning the process of educating them about their problem and its management.

This is an approach to life that is often endorsed by the business community. There is a school of thought about businesses that they, in general, and their employees in particular, do best if they are performing more than half their tasks with mediocrity. This frees up energy and attention for the most important things.

I once heard a similar argument for why we shouldn't vote. An uninformed vote puts us at risk for a bad outcome. It takes time to become informed. The time spent becoming informed must compete with everything else we might do that serves our interests. One vote has a very tiny effect on the outcome, and therefore, very possibly, the tiniest effect on our interests. Now, I'm not saying that we shouldn't vote. What I *am* saying is that all such questions deserve a little more complexity of thought than what Chesterfield exhibited.

It was with some pleasure that I discovered that Samuel Johnson reportedly said of Chesterfield, "This man I thought had been a Lord among wits; but I find he is only a wit among Lords!"

Of course, most people concerned with doing all things well aren't genuinely concerned with the outcome of the thing; they are concerned with the management of their self-esteem.

My father would spend hours and hours in his shop working on carpentry projects. Believe me, they turned out good. The required focus took his mind away from the possibility of looking inward. He experienced this as a comforting refuge. That is, unless he made a mistake. Nothing in the universe could provoke more uncontrolled anger behavior from him than that. The pleasant fantasy of perfection had been breached. Until that moment, he was sure that, if he was doing something, he was doing it well.

I have met many people who have "not competent enough" in their lineup of suspects that explains their unworthiness. It's like self-esteem tetherball: for them, only the most competent person wins. They therefore waver in the face of uncertain competence.

I once spoke with a fellow who was quite tempted to be hard on himself because he wasn't sure he knew how to write a good note of condolence to a friend grieving the death of his father. I have talked with untold sufferers of grief over the years and I am persuaded that the skill in question is one of the rarest (and least practiced) of all. Our society has a collective, shame-based phobia about grief (more on this later). Of course, most of us are going to be unskilled at writing such notes.

I have even met people who, upon hearing my ideas about things, are tempted to be ashamed that they have been "found out" as less competent in the domain of idea development.

In the chapters on laziness and obesity we reviewed how some of us use the belief in superiority as a self-esteem management strategy. The same holds true for competence.

When I was in medical school I watched a partial liver resection (the patient needed to have a piece of his liver removed). The liver is riddled with hundreds of blood vessels. Every one of them had to be tied off when it was severed. A third-year resident was tying the knots. The attending physician criticized every one. Each one was either too tight or too loose. It went on for hours. It is just a small example of the suffering inherent in the way we train physicians. We should see this scene as nothing more than an exercise in sado-masochism (without any "safe" word). If the knots were insufficient, it would have been malpractice not to re-do them.

Why is it like this? Few doctors will admit it; but it is, at least in part, motivated by a wish to instill in the emerging physician, the belief that he has extreme capability. The belief is seared in by hardship. It engenders and perpetuates the belief that the physician has knowledge and abilities that merit high compensation. The guild that is medicine benefits from this.

It is like the "esprit de corps" building the military does. I knew a fellow who went to the Military Academy at West Point. He had so much difficulty satisfying the exacting standards applied to bed making that he never again slept in his bed after he was finally judged to have adequately completed the task. For any task that you can imagine, the newbie will be harshly judged to be a failure. At the end of the trial by hardship, tasks that would have been judged to be failures are judged to be brilliant successes (sometimes without regard to the actual outcome). This produces "the few, the proud." These are the ingredients of the "right stuff."

Confidence is a trait that can be quite useful to a physician or an officer. But it is a tough beast to master. Often, confidence evolves into arrogance. The person with special skills comes to believe they are a superior person.

I think of all this as a self-esteem management strategy we can call "criterion based superiority." Lots of people employ this. They pick a criterion - one they possess, of course - and then use that criterion as proof they are superior to others. The criterion could be wealth, or taste, or fitness, or piloting skills, or educational degree achieved, or college attended, or famous ancestor, or… whatever. I've known PhD's who, through the power of their degree, were certain they had perfect knowledge in every field of study (and most certainly, mine). There are those without degrees at all, who deride those with "book learnin'" and hold to the criterion of "common sense."

Any belief in superiority is, of course, unsupportable by logic. If we happen to possess a skill or trait in abundance - luck, alone, accounts for it. But, more importantly, this is a self-esteem management strategy that harms the user (and us). It must be rigidly and doggedly tended. This soaks up energy that could be much more usefully employed. It blinds the user to anything they might learn from the "inferiors."

Strangely enough, I recently witnessed a perfect melding of the physician and military systems and the self-esteem damage they caused. There recently was an article on a medical news website reporting on a move to *increase* the hours that interns work. In the comments section I wrote of the self-esteem psychology in play behind this sadistic idea. This was a response to my comment: "Are you going to say that by working extremely hard at the University of Pittsburg and then joining the US Army Medical Corps makes me less than you because I have a fragile self-esteem? Go back and read your "Psychology Today" article."

No. I'm not better than you. And you obviously do have a fragile, shame-based self-esteem that is focused on concerns about just who *is* better than who. Such people are like the evil queen in Snow White: forever at their mirror; forever taking down challengers to their superiority.

Many of us who will never know extreme competence are drawn to it by proxy. We are drawn to displays of it like a moth to a flame. Every four years, you will hear people say they don't know why they watch the Olympics, but they still do. Of course, there is drama and patriotism; but - most of all - it's the perfect 10 or the fastest, strongest, best... hopefully, *of all time*.

With such events, we are always distracted by stories of how certain athletes have made a hash of their lives (or, of how certain countries have made a hash of their athletes). Is it not obvious that the collective lust for excellence begets these tragedies?

In the movie "Whiplash" the character, Terence Fletcher, sadistically drives his music students towards a fantasy of perfect competence. In one scene, he insists that his drummer is either rushing or dragging the tempo. It's either one or the other. It is never right.

His justification for behavior like this was, "I was there to push people beyond what is expected of them. Otherwise, we are depriving the world of the next Louis Armstrong, the next Charlie Parker."

Louis Armstrong had multiple failed marriages; an addiction to pot and an eating disorder. Charlie Parker was addicted to heroin and alcohol and died at 34.

Our instinct for perfection is titillated by excellence. It makes us feel like there is a chance for us. The possibility that we might never hear another Charlie Parker or see another Ryan Lochte causes us to feel as though we will have lost so very much. Just possibly, if we could put things into a different perspective, we will have gained so much more.

There are practical reasons for wanting to be good at things. If I'm good at my job it serves your interests and it serves mine. But trying to be the best at one thing probably does not serve a lot of our interests very well at all. The opportunity costs are too great. The risk for anxiety and depression should we fail is too high. We might be happiest if we were content to be a jack of some trades and a journeyman of a few more.

The title of my book may be a rush for some and a drag for others. The same is true of its execution. Indeed, I considered many forms of just those last two sentences. They all had the potential to rush or drag. I know there are objectively derivable errors in the writing. Sometimes, it may have seemed like random chance alone could have led to better punctuation!

I worked pretty hard on this. I could have worked harder. It seems important that it have warts. I could have had professional editing, but that would have made it inauthentic. Prettier, but not me. And, more importantly, inconsistent with the message.

If we were all *content* to be mediocre or poor at most things (which is our destiny) and pretty good at a handful of things, we would, collectively, be in a much better position to attend to all the problems we face. The preoccupation with competence individually can undermine our competence collectively. This may be what we gain if we lose the next Charlie Parker.

We had our own, definitive example of the sado-masochistic, trial-by-suffering event in my psychiatry residency. We residents called it "degradation rounds." This event would occur after we finished a night on-call at the large inner city public hospital that was one of the training sites used by the program. A certain attending physician, whose name will remain anonymous, insisted on having breakfast with us. It was just the two of us.

"Rounding" involves visiting one's patients in turn. It can be literal, or figurative. This was an example of the latter. The attending would review the cases we had seen during the night. He would review the patient's charts and our notes. Then he would criticize. It was a truly mean-spirited affair. The man acted like he was venting years of bitter disappointment upon us.

As luck would have it, my last degradation round was after my busiest night ever. I had seen over a dozen patients and admitted eight of them. By comparison, a typical "bad" night might yield three or four admissions. It was a lot of work. Potentially, it was a target-rich environment for the attending.

He tried hard to find fault; he pulled out all the stops. It didn't matter. By that point I could see through it. When I asked myself the question, "What does this behavior say about him?" the answer was plain enough: his self-esteem required a vampire-like feeding of proof that he had superior competence. He needed to be the Charlie Parker of psychiatry.

I'm afraid it was a bad morning for him. He struggled to find stuff. With each chart, he became more and more obviously desperate for a coup. I think he also became more and more clearly aware that I was onto the game; that he couldn't make me feel small.

I can be measured on a scale of competence in psychiatry... and in canoe paddling and parenting and in a million things I know nothing about. Luck has decided where I land on such scales. I may get better at some. Eventually, I will be able to do none.

The humble self-esteem, truly, is the only one that is invulnerable.

I live about 500 miles to the east of where I trained. On occasion, a passer-by will ask if I have ever bumped into "Dr. Charlie". I will answer, "No... but when the wind is right, I can smell his ego."

Love

My wife used to fart when she was nervous. She had all sorts of wonderful idiosyncrasies. She used to fart in her sleep... One night it was so loud it woke the dog up. She woke up and went, "ah was that you?" I didn't have the heart to tell her.
Sean Maguire in "Good Will Hunting"

I now want to take a departure from the rehabilitation of the usual character suspects. I am hoping that, by now, you are getting the gist of things. I want to write about love, because common beliefs about romantic love are among the things that make us the most miserable. Perhaps, it will not be surprising that the perfection instinct is again at work in this.

Let me summarize part of what we have covered. We come into the world expecting things to be perfect. We expect to be utterly, perfectly adored. Some of us are disappointed of this in a traumatic way. We are made to feel insecure. We tend to blame ourselves for this. We hope to find compensatory adoration from others.

What could be a more perfect solution to a perfect wish than to find the perfect, complimentary soulmate?

This is what many of us set out to do. It is not totally conscious. Remember, instincts run on automatic pilot; just like how we don't have to consciously conjure up our fears about death. As we go through childhood and adolescence we work on the construction of a template for the perfect other; the one that will complete us; the one that will return us to the nirvana state of perfection where we will be free from insecurity.

At some point along the way, we may bump into somebody who seems to fit the template remarkably well. It is so terribly exciting. It's like finding an oasis after a march through the desert. If we also seem to fit that person's template, we will fall head over heels in love. Unfortunately, it usually is all a mirage.

The plan has been to disprove that we are unlovable by finding someone to love us. It is so very tempting to think that we can learn about our value from the subjective opinions of others. But aside from that issue, the plan is just about as inefficient and flawed as it could be.

Let's begin with the inefficiency inherent in the plan. Consider just how different romantic love is from the love of a parent (or, the missing love for which we seek compensation). First of all, parental love has so much more biology going for it. The mother has had the experience of carrying the child within her and then giving birth. While not foolproof, there is a lot to that (including the workings of various hormones) which promotes a bond of attachment. Genetics work so that children will generally look very much like their fathers. This is what ropes them in (the "chip off the old block" thing). With romantic love, there is little more biology at work than sexual attraction. This is a factor that seems to lead down many paths besides love.

We are drawn to the helplessness of the child. We are instinctually drawn to the facial features it shares with kittens and puppies, etc. Caretaking can lead to a sense of investment. We may enjoy the narcissistic pleasure of shaping the child as it develops. We may entertain fantasies of legacy embodied by our children.

Now, let's contrast that with romantic love. Each of us has a range of tolerances that act as screeners of prospective partners. The "screening tool" is part of our template. The screeners may evaluate any number of things: gender, appearance, sexual activity preferences, age, values, interests, intellect, tastes, and money – to name just some. Much of the series, "Seinfeld," was predicated on Jerry's weekly discovery of how a prospective romantic interest got caught by a screen (in one episode the woman's hands were too "mannish"). Some people can have inclusive screens while some can be very particular. Some may have just one or two criteria that kick people out. The bottom line is – most screening tools kick out way more than they let in.

Now let's consider the fact that every prospective partner has their own screening tool. It will be a compendium of their personal preferences. For everybody that makes it through our screen, it is more likely than not that we will not make it through their screen. It's a Venn diagram with very little overlap.

I have run a thought exercise with many patients. I have asked them to name the person they think of as the most eligible. Then, I ask them to think of reasons why someone wouldn't want to be with that person. No matter what, it is easy to come up with many.

I have conducted a thought exercise of my own. At any one time, the college I attended had around 600 female students (noteworthy because of my gender preference screen). When I consider my own idiosyncratic preferences for women, and then consider the likelihood that one of them would have a "taste" for my very particular idiosyncrasies – I can't imagine that there were ever more than 2 or 3 potential matches that would have worked. It was a miracle that I found my wife.

That's just it! These are tremendously long odds to hang our self-esteem hopes on - even if it were a valid way of establishing our lovability. And, to the extent that we are using this plan, we are going to feel crushing rejection when things don't click. We will be discouraged and won't be able to run very many candidates through the screener. The odds then become astronomical. It will be like fishing without a pole and hoping that the fish of our dreams decides to jump into the boat!

There are some who only employ one screen – "I will take the person who loves me." A person can be so desperate to ease their self-doubts and insecurity that they will take anyone. I remember once begging my father to divorce my mother. Remember, he was the "most, well-adjusted person that had ever been born." His response to me was that, were he to ever become separated from my mother, he would have no choice but to commit suicide. This was not a reflection of his attachment to her, but rather to a very limited (wire mesh?) security blanket.

There can be much resistance to the new idea that we can't learn about our lovability from the subjective opinions of others. Sometimes we have endured so much pain and invested so much hope in the possibility that relief will be found in the words, "I love you." We are bombarded by a popular culture that pushes this idea on us, continuously – from Cinderella to Bella Swan and thousands of characters in between.

I know a woman who found romance for the first time a little later in life. She wasn't sure about the fellow though. There was the possibility of character qualities that were inconsistent with her values. She also wasn't sure of herself. She had strong doubts about her lovability and was terribly tempted to think she could have them removed by committing to the relationship. Part of her knew it was wise to hold back a little and learn more about the fellow; but her fears that her hopes would be disappointed made her miserable. In the end, she decided it couldn't work out. The courage that woman displayed was so very impressive.

The "do you love me" screening plan flirts with so many forms of disaster! First of all, there are a good many people out there who would like to exploit us and they know one of their best tickets in is to say that they love us. I have known so many people who become trapped in miserable stories where this is the first chapter. The stories are then sustained by their use of reaction formation; the anticipation of grief should the relationship fail; and their omnipotent fantasy that the exploiter can be changed.

Even if the partner is not an exploiter, relationships based of this screening plan are often very troubled. The partner will find that they are being used as a barometer. Every action they take is carefully measured for what it seems to say about the lovability of the other. The measurers will find themselves perpetually choosing behaviors that they anticipate will induce the partner to offer up another feeding of affirmation. And when the feedings are too infrequent, the frustrated wishes for affirmation may spur a host of invective and punishment that corrodes the relationship. It easy to see that there is no real love here at all.

In popular culture, love stories are said to go like this – boy meets girl, boy loses girl, boy regains girl. It must be that there is something very important to the human psyche that this plot is so common. It is a plot that leads us to a true understanding of romantic love.

When two templates do manage to overlap, it is terribly exciting. The bulk of all popular literature about love is about this. In the Twilight Saga, we are led down the very pleasant narrative; that this is a state that can go on... forever. Maybe... but not likely. Despite our wishes and instincts to the contrary, templates probably never perfectly overlap. As time passes, the elements that are missing from our template become more and more apparent.

What follows is what I think of as the "Hunter's Dilemma." Where I am from one can hunt for one deer and one elk, only, during a defined "season." At the beginning of the season it seems like there will be lots of opportunity to find the animal of one's dreams. The hunter has a mental template for just what that animal will be like. At any point in the season, should the hunter see an animal that doesn't match the template, a decision must be made: go with this one or take the chance that a better one will come.

And this is how boy loses girl. The cracks in the template become too great. Either boy or girl decides to take a chance on another opportunity. But, sometimes... boy regains girl! Sometimes we can decide to forego the template. We can decide to love another for just exactly who they are. This is what the Robin Williams character was getting at in "Good Will Hunting". This is what real romantic love is and it is some of the rarest stuff around.

My wife tends to leave the bread sack open. She tends to exaggerate. She has tended to react to my enthusiasm with caution (in my less wise days, my feelings would be hurt). These are not, necessarily, traits I would search for in another, but I hope my wife never changes. These are among the traits that make her the unique person who has been such a lucky blessing to me.

Real love requires that we deal with our primary insecurity by looking inward. This frees us up to see another for who they really are. A patient recently told me the following story: He and his wife had visited neighbors. An impassioned conversation about politics ensued. Afterward, the wife, who had not joined in the argument, told my patient he had behaved like an ass. The patient checked his impulse to take offense and considered his wife. She had come from a background that promoted a good deal of insecurity about relationships. She was sensitive to any possibility that aggression could cause hurt feelings and distance in a relationship. The patient reviewed the events; confirmed that he had been vigilant for signs that things were getting out of hand; and then viewed his wife's behavior with compassion.

My patient demonstrated the vital skill of empathy. It is a skill that we can only develop after we have dealt with our primary insecurity. It is the mechanism by which we can we see other people for who they truly are. It requires that we set aside the "what does this say about me?" questions in favor of the "what does this say about them?" questions.

People often confuse empathy for sympathy. Empathy is seeing through another's eyes in a way that allows us to predict and understand their responses to things. Let me give an example. Why are there a lot of dead skunks on the highway (if you live in a place where there are not skunks you must trust me on this)? It's because, for its whole life, whenever anything approached the skunk, it stopped. Therefore, the skunk has every reason to expect that the same holds true for the car. I just empathized with a skunk! (not a common subject of our sympathies!)

If I had said a dog had been hit on the highway, chances are, you would have had an emotional reaction. You may have memories of your own experiences with dogs. The more your emotions get involved, the harder it is to know whether you are having empathy or sympathy. Sympathy is what we sense we would feel if we were in the same situation as another. People will claim that I couldn't possibly understand what they are going through because I haven't gone through it myself. The opposite is more likely. If I had been through "it" (the experience could never be the same), the experience would be colored by who I am. I am more likely to have sympathy, not empathy. Professional poker players are great at empathy. They are in their opponents' mind and anticipating their moves. If they have any sympathy, they save it for after the game.

This is why empathy is essential if we are to see another, in their true, unvarnished state. Empathy is the essential compass that leads to real love, because it reveals the real person. It also leads to compassion. Empathy takes *us* out of the equation. With empathy and a humble self-esteem, we cannot have hurt feelings.

I knew a woman who firmly believed that she could make her husband love her. At first, she tried to please him. Later, she tried to scold him. It went on for years and she became more and more bitter. It was only after she started working with me that she came to realize that he had no capacity for empathy whatsoever. At no time, had he ever had an accurate view of how his wife was feeling and why. Indeed, he rarely

205

considered the possibility that he should try. All her efforts were no more likely to meet with success than if she were to try to cure a blind child by singing to it. If she had asked "what does this say about him questions; if she had not had her own problems with empathy; if she had not had such a grandiose expectation of her potency – she would have been spared much suffering.

I often tell my patients that real love isn't knowing what your partner's favorite song is – it's knowing *why* it's their favorite song. With real love, we love the real person... and they *know* it's their real self that is being loved.

When love is a lucky thing that does not measure us, we will be less interested in being loved. If it happens, great. The Beatles song says, "And in the end, the love you take is equal to the love you make." I've always been uncomfortable with that sentiment. Without primary insecurity; with a humble self-esteem – there is no need for accounting. We are free to love whoever we want. If it is not returned, there is little harm done.

I recently have been thinking about what should be present in a useful screening tool. These are the ingredients I would recommend to everyone. You could maybe avoid a lot of trouble by using it. Perhaps you will find it a little bit unconventional (but, by now, how surprising would that be!?)

1. Dedication to a 50/50 reciprocal relationship where no one is exploited.

2. Dedication to empathy; to effort that brings understanding.

3. Dedication to compromise when there is disagreement.

4. An appreciation for gratitude – freely given and easily received.

5. Dedication to wisdom when angry.

6. Predisposed to kindness and consideration.

7. Has managed insecurity fairly well.

8. Has complimentary skills.

9. Has compatible interests and values.

10. Knows what real love is.

Sex

*It is necessary for God to awaken people to
a sense of guilt and danger... which will
break the power of carnal and worldly
desire.*
Charles G Finney

*...the female brown trout fakes the trout
equivalent of orgasm. Nobody, probably
least of all the male trout, is sure what
this means.*
The New Yorker

*Dudes, you have got to stop shaming the
women you have casual sex with.*
Priya Alika Elias

*This chapter is about relations between men and women.
Of course, there are other relationships and other
identities I could have considered. The exclusion was not
due to disinterest, but rather a wish for more simplicity
and economy. Where I could have cut a wide swath, I have
hoped to cut a deep channel instead. Believe me, I know
how exclusion feels. Please forgive me.

How can we possibly remove sex from the
lineup of character suspects that undermines our
worthiness? It may seem like nothing leads to
more suffering than the results of our sexual
impulses.

There are a lot of things we have inherited from more primitive species that don't work too well for us. Our spines were invented to be horizontal and any engineer will tell you that the design is very good for the intended purpose. When our ancestors stood up, they had to bring the design with them. The result of using this design for an unintended purpose is low back pain.

The flight or fight response evolved in response to death by predation. It originated in creatures that, compared to us, were pinheads. A massive discharge of adrenaline does everything you could want if you are a shrew being chased by a cat. Adrenaline causes mental confusion in us. In a time of emergency, our inheritance deprives us of our best asset. What does the shrew care?

Sexual impulse worked pretty well for us when we lived in widely dispersed bands. Something had to get males to cross the dangerous hinterland to find mates and avoid interbreeding. But sex is problematic for "civilized" people.

Sexual impulses are like any impulse. Just as with wishes to be aggressive, or dependent, or to want things; we can't judge sexual impulses. We can only judge the behaviors we use to put the impulse into action. We should probably want to learn to be wise about how we put such impulses into action. We need to learn to like our sexual impulses to be wise with them. The problem is, probably more than with any other impulse, there is so much in our way.

The root of the problem is that we don't like each other very much. Not only do we have to manage sexual impulses, but, often, they are mixed with anger impulses. We are bad enough with the two individually. Collectively it has been a disaster. The sexes are now said to be at war. The other day I was trying to make a point with a patient when she burst out with, "Oh, no! You aren't going to make me feel compassion for men, are you?!" Perhaps it was a moment of change exhaustion.

Compassion was precisely what I was attempting. Everybody is playing the best they can at every moment in time, under the circumstances. I must be able to be compassionate in every circumstance. It is not hard with the states of men and women; so, I will attempt it now. Making the case for men might be the more difficult sell, however, so I will start with them.

If we are to understand things in non-shaming, objective terms, we must create a narrative of circumstances. This is just what I have done at other times in this book. As you may have noticed, I have already started this one.

Testosterone makes a lion's mane turn dark and fight for his pride. It makes a bull elk shed the velvet of its antlers and guard his harem. It makes the sage grouse strut in his lek. And it makes us men think about sex... a lot. When I prescribe some antidepressants, I must warn my patients that they may experience a decrease of their libidos. Many men have told me that they would find relief in such a side effect (women are much more inclined to complain about lost libido. But only about half are missing their interest in sex. The others worry that less interest in sex will make them lose their man.).

Testosterone makes male creatures aggressively compete for mates. For most of animal history this meant that the "fittest" male would pass on their genes. We now live in a time when, mostly, such aggression no longer fits. Intelligence, for example, may be a truer test of fitness. And yet, we actively shame weakness and promote aggression.

It is because of testosterone that we invented the vampire myth. The vampire may *seem* powerful, but he is compelled, shallow and hollow. He is ruled by his need for blood.

Sex is a thing that men want that is unlike most other things we want. More than anything else, it involves the feelings of somebody else. Make an unwise choice with sexual desire and there are going to be a lot of hard feelings.

It's too bad men get sexual impulses before they have the chance to be wise. The onset of brain maturation that allows for abstract reasoning arrives too late. Adolescents drive their parents crazy with the foolish things they do. Remember how there may be an evolutionary advantage to the foolishness of adolescents. It may be that sex drive alone isn't enough to get men to cross the hinterlands to seek out other tribes. They may have had to be foolish too.

Perhaps we could aspire for a culture that did all it could to compensate for the wisdom gap of adolescent males. Instead, we do almost everything possible to prevent compensation. As a result, foolish adolescents often just grow up to be foolish men.

Of course, we shame sexual impulses. We shame them to the point where they are often never talked about. We certainly don't talk about how to be wise with them. We shame them to the point where they are acted upon impulsively. There is plenty of evidence that shows that men who actively shame sexual impulses are among the most likely to commit marital infidelity. When the opportunity unexpectedly falls in their lap, they have no wisdom to call upon. Shame decreases the chance that there could be a healthy affiliation between men of different generations that might compensate for foolishness.

Deflected shame creates scenarios where men cannot look inward. They cannot accept the possibility of making a mistake. They always find scapegoats for their unwise behavior choices. They run amok. They create a lot of hard feelings in women.

Deflected shame leads to whole cultures of men who abdicate all responsibility for the management of sexual impulses. Women become the scapegoats. Women are forced to choose behaviors (such as clothing choices) to control men who do not wish to become wise.

Problematic management of insecurity also complicates things. We too often seek to establish our worthiness through affirmation from others. We create idealized templates for the "best" forms of affirmation. Sexual impulse tends to cause men to emphasize sexual attributes when we look for affirmation. When we use other people for affirmation, we turn them into objects. When we emphasize physical attributes when we look for affirmation, we turn them into sex objects.

Sometimes we use criteria to establish our self-esteem. One criterion might be: most conquests of women (or, conquest of the most "desirable" woman). Once again, women are turned into objects. Or, we might conflate sexual prowess with strength. If this is the case, then any talk of how to be wise with the control of sexual impulse may seem like shameful weakness. "Locker room talk" may seem like the safer alternative.

There are large segments of some cultures where such problematic management of self-esteem is the norm. Men will pursue women with tools of seduction that are carefully honed. Once the woman is won over, she then becomes a possession to be jealously guarded. If we aren't careful, women could start to hate us.

In fact, a lot of women do hate us. They see our behaviors without compassion and they feel like victims. Victims tend to see things in black-and-white terms. Men become demonized. Polarization occurs.

Every man has had the experience of approaching a woman and being turned down. Many women have hard feelings towards men. Many women have an ability to turn a man down in remarkably humiliating ways. In an ideal world, the man would not take this personally; he would see it as useful information about the woman (perhaps, disaster averted!). It is not an ideal world. Many men will have hard feelings. Anger enters the equation. In our imperfect world, such feelings are often poorly managed. A sex management problem becomes an anger management problem. More polarization occurs.

It feels like the case for compassion for women hardly needs any effort. They have had a very difficult time. However, perhaps there are a few things to address.

Probably every man has had bad experiences caused by women. There is the possibility of the mother who hates men and takes it out on boys. There is the girl on the playground who is cruel to the shy and insecure. There is the woman who turns us away with sadistic genius. With the mother and the woman, it is a chicken-or-the egg question. Cruelty has begat cruelty forever. With the girl, it isn't about sex, it just sticks in the boy's memory that way. As with most bullies, it is more a matter of "bad stuff" running downhill.

What most gets to men is how women can inflame our sexual impulses. They seem to play into our wish to see them as an object. They go to great effort to tempt us. They tease us. They play into all our terrible strategies for the management of sexual impulse and self-esteem. And then they turn us down. Or worse, they humiliate us. Or worse, they demonize us.

This is not to say that women are responsible for our behavior. It might serve their interests to be wiser with their impulses, however.

Women may play upon our impulses. But if it is "play," they could understandably claim that we established the rules of the game. For most of our history, especially our modern history, men have held most of the political and economic power. We left women who wanted to get ahead no choice but to use the few advantages left to them to become attached to the best man they could get. "Mansplaining" is an example of how this remains alive today.

Women have ambivalence about sex appeal. They sense that it is part of the "game," but they hate to be objects. They may want to attract a partner and yet still want real love. Shame may make them unaware of their sexual impulses and their desire for affirmation. It is small wonder they sometimes give mixed messages. I have known female patients who would dress in provocative ways and yet be shocked at the idea that they could be signaling sexual interest. Mixed messages often lead to hard feelings.

It is sadly ironic that men, by making sex objects of women, have diminished the chances that women will enjoy their sexual impulses and want to have sex with us. Even worse, of course, it makes it impossible for us to love each other.

Problems with insecurity also complicate matters for women. Much too often, they try to quell doubts about their worthiness of love by appealing to a man's lust. They feel that, if a man is attracted to them, they have learned something about their value. They put themselves up as an object. They confuse the actions driven by the man's "little brain" as something to do with love.

The foolishness of adolescence fuels this. You only need to be a chaperone at a high school prom to know that this is true (I wish the efforts that go into making and enforcing high school dress codes would go into classes on self-esteem management!). And yet, this tends to persist very late into life. I once had a woman in her 70's ask me about psychotherapy because she realized that she spent more time thinking about and acting to promote her sexual attractiveness than anything else. She had the courage to admit that this seemed shallow.

Madison Avenue fuels this. It doesn't help that there are a lot of people who want to sell us stuff, who prey upon all these poorly managed impulses.

An idea that summarizes the misfortunate in all this for women is the "revenge body". Some poor shallow fellow dumps you because you are not a good enough sex object... and you strive to prove he was wrong? And we make television about it?!?

As with other polarized situations, we need to find a third path we both can embrace. Things could be different if we took shame out of anger and sex and determined to be wise with them. It is self-evident that respect and compassion are the cornerstones of such wisdom. Things would be different if we managed self-esteem in an enlightened way. We would probably have more love *and* more sex! And the sex would be better too! This should be an easy sell.

It is not until we turn down the third path that we can start to unwind the damage. Then we can own the fact that we have managed our sexual impulses quite foolishly. We can then own that we are hurting each other. Hopefully, we will feel an impulse to apologize. All real apologies include a commitment to behave differently.

There are some things about Stephanie Meyer's depiction of vampires that I'm not crazy about. Some elements are a bit saccharine and some a bit puritanical for my tastes. But I think she provided an interesting model for how things might work better. The Cullens are not ashamed of their lust for human blood (think sex). They openly talk about it. They plan with each other on how to manage it. Their attractions to others seem to be based on true love and not objectification. Even Bella, who seems to have some self-esteem issues at the beginning of the stories, actively seeks to know Edward for who he is, rather than cling to a template of what she wants.

It may seem trite, but the Walt Disney quote applies here: "If you can dream it, you can do it."

Grief

Life is short, shorter for some than for others.
Gus McCray, in "Lonesome Dove"

Old age could be seen as a mixed blessing. I suppose that only then - when, all the time, every day, life is a challenge; when all or most of your peers are gone - perhaps it feels like a person can have had enough life. Until then, life feels short. Gus may have given the shortest eulogy ever, but he nailed it.

As I wrote before, I have had the honor of spending a lot of time with grieving people. I feel the need to emphasize that it is an *honor*. Unfortunately, many of my patients don't see it that way. Too often, they have been twisted to believe that the experience of grief and (even worse) related displays of emotion, are signs of weakness and... you know... weakness must be shameful. How tragic. What an insult to injury. With death and with grief, the perfection instinct again plays havoc with us.

My father had a military funeral. It was an amazing thing to watch. There was so much attention to honor. Honor to the service given. Honor to the loss of one disposed to serve. Honor to the meaning of the loss to those left behind.

At the service, a carefully uniformed man knelt before my mother, presented her with a meticulously folded flag, and spoke of a grateful nation. I keep that flag in my office. It is a reminder that I do not need. It is a symbol for what I try to teach my patients.

Grief is no different from any other impulse or feeling in the sense that we can make no judgements about it until we put it into action. Then, we can judge the behavior in terms of how is serves our interests. Why judge the emotion harshly? That will only drive it into the unconscious. Why not judge it to be honorable?

Before we are born, we are not shown a contract. We never see the necessary language of that contract: "You will expect everything to be perfect and then you will be disappointed of that expectation again and again throughout your life. Furthermore, you will be blind to the fact that the expectation is an illusion and, because of this, your losses will always come as tragically ironic surprises. If you have any feelings about this, most of those you know will shame you."

It would be nice to be shown such a contract. I wonder who would sign it. From this perspective, how can we have anything but compassion for the pain we feel with loss?

When we shame grief, we make the surprises even more likely and painful. We cannot sit with our grief until the last irrevocable moment. When my grandmother died at the age of 99, after years and years of dementia, it could not have been more obvious that her non-existence could have been anticipated. It could even be argued that there had been little or no existence for a good long while. Yet, my mother was shattered; gob smacked.

There are ways of putting grief into action that do serve our interests. They require that we do not view grief as shameful. They require that we see the perfection instinct for what it is. The first thing we can employ is gratitude.

I once spoke with a patient who was contemplating leaving town for a vacation. But there was a catch: there was a frail elderly friend to be left behind. It was not certain that the friend would die anytime soon. But my patient was beside herself with the logistical problem of how to make certain she could stay informed of the friend's status and how to rush to the bedside for the last moment, should it come.

When I asked her how she felt about grief she gave the expected answer – it was a horrible thing and a shameful sign of weakness. It was something to be avoided with vigor.

I suggested to her that if grief was not shameful, then she could enjoy the benefits of gratitude. She could be keenly aware that each and every moment she spends with her friend could be the last. She would not take the moment for granted, but would be grateful for it. She would be more present in the moment and, at the last, would feel satisfied that it was a moment well spent. And, when the last moment came, there would be no panic. After all, what can you expect? Life is short.

What can you expect? That question relates to the second adaptive thing we can do with our grief: we can work to reach acceptance of the loss. I can't tell you how often I have suggested this and found only blank-eyed incredulity for a response. Is such a thing possible?

Here is perhaps the cruelest handiwork of the perfection instinct. We are disinclined to believe that bad things can happen to us. If we ever come to accept that they can, it usually only comes afterwards. But why not get to work on it now? The bad stuff is inevitable.

I suspect one of the most difficult sermons to write is "Why do bad things happen to good people?" But it is only hard to the extent that we avoid the answer: shit happens.

I said that crudely to shock the senses. It is so very hard to accept that we could be subject to random bad luck. Our instincts tell us we are too important for that to happen.

A gamma ray passes through a man's frontal lobe. It causes chromosomal damage. A faulty gene then begins coding for the machinery of a tumor. The tumor destroys the man's judgement and his capacity to regulate emotion. He climbs a clock tower and massacres innocent people. It's all completely random. You can create a similar objective narrative to explain all the shit that happens in the world.

The other day I was driving on a dirt road winding through a mountain forest. I rounded a bend and, right in the middle of the road, I saw the largest, most magnificent bull elk I have ever seen. What a marvelous, coincidental intersection of agendas that was!

A half hour before, on the highway, I narrowly missed being in a horrific traffic accident. At another place and time random coincidence may have led me not to an elk, but to an infected mosquito, or an IED.

The fact that random bad shit just happens may be the hardest of all the weird things I have asked you to believe. We want things to make sense, but the sense we want is ruled by grandiose fantasies driven by instinct. We do not want to think that our lives are ruled by randomness. It is too humbling. In fact, it can be terrifying to think we could be so insignificant. This is perhaps much worse than accepting that the earth rotates before an insignificant sun.

We have been set up, by instinct, to suffer greatly. There is such a wide gulf between what we expect and what we find. Just as with anger, this difference is the measure of the grief we are destined to experience. Acceptance is how we close the gap and find peace. This is much better than maintaining falsehoods that cause our wounds to fester.

We all have practiced acceptance without much notice. In childhood, grandiosity causes us to have fantasies of how our lives might turn out that fail to materialize. Again and again, we must say to ourselves, "I guess I'm just not going to get to have that kind of life."

I once spoke with a man who said he was feeling guilty about neglecting his mother. He felt he should be calling her more often. He kept insisting that he loved his mother.

I asked about his mother; about any criteria by which she might have earned his love. On every account, she had failed spectacularly. I had heard a lot of stories of neglect, but this one was without peer.

I suggested to the man that his guilt was mostly based on his failure to accept reality; his failure to grieve the fact that he had one of those lives in which his one and only mother was unworthy of love. He had one of those lives where he would never experience a mother's love. He hadn't wanted to give up the hope that this was untrue. Acceptance, however, would free him to see the true nature of the relationship; and his judgements about it would be wiser and more comfortable.

We need to grieve the disappointments our lives bring. Perhaps, especially those brought by our parents. Our parents can make this very difficult. We naturally want to idealize them. I can't tell you of the sort of underserving fellows I've heard described as the "greatest daddy in the world."

When I was in my psychotherapy I started out with great guilt about the feelings I was discovering about my childhood. I felt like a traitor to the idealized image I had of my father. My therapist told me about a cartoon he had seen in a magazine: Two men were sitting on a park bench. The first one asks, "How is your psychotherapy going?" The second answers, "Great! It's just been a month and I already hate my parents!"

This sort of guilt is made so very worse if our parents need to be idealized; need to see themselves as perfect. Not only does this tend to provide them with an introspection-free pass to engage in the very worst kinds of parenting, but they will insist that it is all perfectly normal. As I said before, they will engage us in what we can call a "reality battle". We may have strong feelings that what we are being subjected to is just not right, but they just go on insisting that it is. If you have been subject to a reality battle, psychotherapy could be very helpful for sorting out the truth.

I have known several people who have put their grief into counterproductive action. They avoided gratitude and acceptance.

There was the mother who, following the death of her son, locked his room and never went back in until she met me 10 years later.

There was the woman who had the uncanny knack for identifying dates on the calendar that were important anniversaries connected to the death of her sister. Each one led to a re-experiencing of debilitating pain. They also kept the woman rooted in the past and (in her mind) excused from dealing with an uncertain future.

There was the man who put his head down and went back to work after he lost his son. He was determined to act as he felt he must. He wondered why he had so much trouble with his temper.

There was the woman who was always on the go. She could never slow down. She even talked fast. It was as though she was always on the run from her painful past.

Each of these people finally found peace when they were guided to acceptance.

When it comes to acceptance, the reality that we are going to die may be the greatest challenge. The prospect of our non-existence makes us quake and quail. This is one piece of evidence that the survival instinct and the perfection instinct are one in the same.

The fact of non-existence offends our wish for importance. Instinct makes it hard to be so humble. When I first heard of Michael Heizer's sculpture called "Levitated Mass", a 340-ton rock, I thought, "This man craves permanence!"

From the very beginning; from a time when we could not possibly have understood the workings of instinct; we have created myths that let us avoid consideration of the possibility that we might not exist. Such is the terrible nature of the prospect. Such is our thrall to the perfection instinct.

A little over 100 years ago my great grandfather was the governor of a state. Maybe that's a pretty big deal. It was just a blink in time ago. I very much doubt that there is anybody on the planet who knows more about him than I do. I could not write, from my own knowledge, more than a thousand words about him. When I am gone, the world's leading expert won't be able to write a hundred.

But it is *worse* than that. Consider love. We can't be said to be loved unless we are truly known. Otherwise, we are just being seen as an object. Remember, love isn't knowing someone's favorite song; it's knowing *why* it is their favorite song. I don't know any of the "whys" that affected my great grandfather. He is just an object to me. He does not even exist in memory.

We can make a big rock. We can put our name on a building. We can do famous things. Ultimately, we will not exist; not even in memory. We are never more important than a grain of sand on an infinite beach.

Friends have expressed the concern that I have used too many contemporary references in this book. They fear that it won't be too long before they lose relevance for the reader. Romney, Lochte, Winfrey, Armstrong, Woods, Kwan, so many Kardashians – how ironic that such people, who have spent so much effort trying to achieve lasting fame, should be considered Achilles' heals, undermining this books legs.

The match is not the miracle; it is the flame. All this effort of mine can hope to do is bring life to an ember. In no time at all, I will not exist in memory, but perhaps the idea will. Lao Tzu does not exist in memory; but his ideas have lived for 1500 years.

If you would like nonexistence to be less distressing -- enlightenment and the humble self-esteem can help. With the humble self-esteem, there is the realization that we all have the same value all the time. With this, the whole question of self-esteem becomes moot and uninteresting. The mind is freed up to think about more useful things. Non-existence is easier to take as self becomes less important; as self takes its appropriate place in reality. I don't know if the meek will inherit the earth, but they have a pretty good gig.

Once, I was talking to my son, when I had a short seizure. From my perspective, there he was and then, there he was. I had no notion of the 30 seconds that intervened. During that time my brain was completely unplugged. Everything about my existence was shut down. I had been gone. The experience was just as I imagined it would be. I found that surprisingly comforting.

The Wilderness

Here we find nature to be the circumstance which dwarfs every other circumstance, and judges like a god all men who come to her.
Ralph Waldo Emerson

The other night I had a dream. They say that nobody likes to hear about another person's dream, but please bear with me. There was a time when dreams were thought of as the window to the universe.

I had been tasked to create a reality TV show connected to my book. Unencumbered by the sense of the ridiculous that would have greeted such a mission in my waking hours, I went right to work. I determined that the show would involve three participants. They would be brought to the wilderness. The main purpose for this – the words came quite clearly to me – "so that they would discover their place."

I mean place like rank or station. Before I can elaborate on why this is important, I want to summarize some of what we have been covering. Humans have a survival instinct. An instinct is an inherited impulse to act that does not involve reasoning. The period of time when we could make the best use of such an instinct is when we are quite young and cannot think strategically. Instincts cannot be turned off and are not necessarily rational (like my cat burying a felt mouse in her food bowl).

An essential element of our survival instinct is a sense of importance. Babies need to put themselves first. This sense of importance affects us throughout our lives and has affected us throughout our history. It has caused us to have exceptionally high expectations of ourselves. There was a long time when we just knew that the earth was the center of the universe. There was a long time when we just knew that humans were so superior to animals that we could not possibly have evolved from them. Our gods tend to be personally involved in providing for our needs.

The instinct therefore makes us think in terms of hierarchy. We put our gods in the sky. Kings and Popes are on the best of terms with them. Good is up and bad is down. It's not just cleanliness that is next to godliness – all "goodliness" is next to godliness.

When I was younger and more foolish, I was keenly aware of my "status" while driving. There are about 70 miles of two lane highway between my house and the house of my in-laws. If someone passed me on the highway, I felt diminished. If I passed someone, I felt exalted. It's a wonder I am still alive.

But we do this all the time. The other day a patient told me about her rehabilitation from a hip replacement. By all objective measures, she was doing well. But she was unhappy. She had been comparing herself to others and felt she was coming up shamefully short. Many patients have told me that they hate going to the gym because they feel compelled to compare this or that body part with the people they see there. Study subjects can be asked to do the most trivial of things – like playing tiddlywinks – and everyone will be keenly aware of their status within the group. Being at the bottom of a totem pole can be very stressful. But being at the top and facing the prospect of losing to an inferior is perhaps the most stressful situation of all.

So where does the wilderness feature in this? The point I want to make is that, for a long time, we have struggled with it for our place. As Emerson points out above, the wilderness is a tough environment. It might be better than us. This has been a critical factor that has had a continuing effect on our culture and ourselves.

We create myths related to hierarchy. They come from how we feel about our place. We can decide that Kings have divine rights. We can decide that one race or gender is superior to another. We can decide that merit should decide what we get out of life (even when the merits are attributable to luck alone).

When we determine that something is higher on the totem pole than us, we become uneasy and ambivalent about it. Tom Brady and LeBron James have fans and haters in nearly equal measures. We create superheroes, so that we can vicariously experience the powers we don't possess and then create supervillains to take them down a peg. We have political parties that champion the little guy and scapegoat the strong and others that do the opposite.

I know, for a fact, that the wilderness is my better. This is how I learned it. When I was 13, I went on my first week-long hike around Mount Rainier. I was one of the youngest and smallest on the trip. I was engulfed by the 40-pound pack on my back. Every day, I fell hopelessly behind most of the others. As is my way, I determined I must establish a strategy for coping with this.

I became "he who endures". I would be the one who puts his head down and just keeps going. Sometimes I would catch up to the lead boys, because they had been resting and lollygagging. They would see me and get up and race off. There would be no rest for me. I was "he who endures".

Being "he who endures" can be a coping strategy that works well in a lot of situations, but not all. When I was 17, I again set off on the week-long hike around Mount Rainier. Now it was I who was amongst the biggest and strongest in the group. I had had a good deal of training in wilderness survival. Some of the knowledge, however, was no more than theoretical.

The hardest day of the hike was a stretch of over 10 miles with the last 8 being a steady, steep, uphill grind. The weather was terrible: driving rain lashed by 30 mph winds. But I was "he who endures". I put my head down. I was keeping warm, because I was working my body so hard. When I finally arrived at the day's destination, I was far, far ahead of everyone else in the group...

Not long ago, I found myself watching a honey bee investigate a columbine flower. Suddenly, it became frozen in place. I looked closer and discovered that, what both the bee and I had believed to be the pillars of the flower, were, in fact, the translucent-white legs of a crab spider. The camouflage had been exquisite. The poison sting had done its work. How remarkable. Over the span of uncountable years the bee and the flower had worked out this symbiotic relationship. All the while, the spider had been working out a way to exploit them both. Such is the awesome beauty and the awesome heartlessness of nature.

... and so it was, on that bitterly cold, windswept ridge, between and above the flow of two glaciers, that the white legs of death reached out for me. As soon as I stopped hiking, my body temperature plummeted. I had never know such shivering. There was no shelter from the wind. I would have to put up my tarp. When I tried to work my fingers, I discovered that the paralyzing

sting of hypothermia had begun its work on me.
I could hardly make my hands do anything. I
really had to be "he who endures" then.
Methodically and painstakingly I worked out the
knots that normally would have taken a second.
I got out my backpacking stove and made some
soup. Another half mile of hiking or 5 degrees
less temperature and I might not be writing this.

When we lived in small bands that
survived by hunting and gathering, we knew our
place. It was the place of the dependent and the
subject. The wilderness was our mother and was
imbued with our gods.

As we advanced into herding and farming,
we approached the status of rivals with the
wilderness. Our feelings became more mixed.
Depending on circumstance, the wilderness may
have been home to the noble savage or the heart
of darkness.

When it became clear that we could be the
master of wilderness, we have taken on the
haughtiness of masters. Wilderness became
something to be exploited for our benefit. Once
the noble savage had his land taken and his
population decimated, he was demoted to mere
savage. We even appropriated his name for our
sports teams, adorned ourselves with his
attributes and wondered: why does he complain.
It was, after all, a contest. He lost. Why is he
such a sore loser?

And now our haughtiness has brought us to the brink. I live in a forest. Every year there are fewer trees. The pine beetle is killing them. The change in climate has brought the pine beetle. Every year, I strive to save my trees, but I know it is a futile effort. There will be a day in the not too distant future when the hillside will be as empty as Tiny Tim's carefully preserved chair.

The notion of climate change has thrown a monkey wrench into our comfortable belief in our dominance. We are treating the fact of it with a petulance ill-befitting our presumed status. And some of us are just plain treating it with denial. The United States Congressman, Tim Walberg, recently said of climate change, "I believe there is a creator God who is much bigger than us. And I'm confident that, if there is a real problem, He can take care of it"

Such is the grip that our instinctual expectation of importance has on us. It is the same grip that entranced Moctezuma at the coming of Cortez. It is becoming the grip of the white spider.

The fact of the matter is, climate change is a problem right now. Thousands are dying as a result of it – through numerous forms of natural disaster – right now. God seems to have his hands in his pockets.

My trees are dying. The left hand of our government doesn't seem to know what the right hand is doing. The left hand wants to be the dominant master and treat the trees of the wilderness as a crop. The right hand wants to exploit other resources of nature in such a way that the crop will certainly be destroyed. I will hear apologists for climate change deniers make their "intellectual" arguments for doing nothing. They will say that the harm done in the future is theoretical, while the harm done to humans in the present, should we do something, is certain. Humans should be so important. By the same logic, we should never save for our children's college or our own retirements. We would never take care of our homes. We would never be stewards of our land.

The instinctual inclination toward hierarchy is making it impossible to rise to the greatest challenge of our times. We must come at this problem with more humility. If we could think more horizontally, we could reconnect with the interdependence we have with nature and wilderness. We are lost; led astray by our instincts. Thoreau said, "Not until we are lost do we begin to understand ourselves. And not until we are completely lost, or turned around, - do we appreciate the vastness and strangeness of nature."

I have been so blessed with opportunities to appreciate wilderness. It is an appreciation that has come as much from the lab and textbook as the field and forest. I know my place, but I'm precocious. I love to test myself against nature; flirt with her forbearance. But I have learned that I must do much more than endure. I must take care. It is the home of the flower and the bee... and the spider. I must watch for the signs and, sometimes, topple my king.

All this has helped me in my work. More than anything, it has helped me see the role that instinct plays in our lives.

I was once with a man hunting antelope. We were sitting on the side of small half-pipe valley. We saw antelope walking towards us from about 200 yards below. We kept still and they took no notice of us. One by one, they walked by us in single file. Finally, after about twenty had filed by, up came an old buck. The hunter shot him.

I had expected that the sound of the shot would send the rest of the antelope in a frenzied gallop over the ridge at the end of the valley. I found what happened instead to be quite remarkable. The antelope formed a circle around the fallen. They stood there, looking at him, for several seconds. Then, there was a sharp bark and the antelope ran off over the ridge, following a new leader.

I have often thought that there could be a tremendous impulse to anthropomorphize such an event. We tend to see ourselves as so important. How better to see a story than through our own lens? Surely, the antelope must have been memorializing the best among them...

I have a slightly different slant on the impulse to anthropomorphize. Consider a sentient antelope reviewing the state of humans. Could it not say, "Look at how preoccupied they are with issues of self-esteem. Look at how preoccupied they are with their sense of place. See how so much of their behavior is driven by instinct. They are so much like us!"

Enlightenment

Knowing others is wisdom,
knowing yourself is enlightenment.
Lao Tzu

Some may aspire to new ideas. I rather enjoy stumbling upon ideas that are quite old. Take Lao Tzu, for example. I've never been a student his ideas. I'm comfortable admitting that I am no expert in many things and that the list includes Eastern religion and philosophy in general and popular notions of enlightenment in particular.

My path has been one of self-reliance and distrust in authority (I wouldn't necessarily recommend this path, it's just the one that got me here). I find it exciting to discover that an idea I have been tossing around aligns with one that is 1500 years old. It feels like I am onto something that probably has some truth in it.

Both Lao Tzu and I suggest the same path. We encourage you to look inward. I encourage you to look for automatic, counterproductive patterns of behavior; to look for the beliefs that drive them; to see the influence of the perfection instinct. I have tried to help the process by taking the sting of shame out of it and by showing you what to look for.

Enlightenment is a delightful word. Rarely does a homonym exploit both of its

meanings at once. Enlightenment brings light –
understanding. Enlightenment takes away
suffering – it diminishes our burdens.

I have read more on the subject now that I
have arrived at this chapter. My humble take on
the traditional, Eastern, notion of enlightenment
is that the following elements lie at its core:

- It is a process by which suffering is
  diminished.
- Discomfort with self is the source if
  suffering.
- Sources of discomfort with self include:
  shame, insecurity, blame, guilt, pride
  and expectation.

If you look, you can see the workings of the
perfection instinct in the traditional model of
enlightenment. This shouldn't be surprising.
The origins of these beliefs are from a time when
there could be no understanding of instinct. For
example, the Buddha is generally said to be
interested in the *elimination* of suffering. This is
a dangerous notion. It temps the pilgrims on the
enlightenment path to think that there is
something shamefully deficient about them,
because they still suffer.

I don't think we can get to such a perfect
place, and only suffer more if we try. I suppose
instinct inspires us to want to look *up* to
someone. If we were all content to be mediocre,
we would have to get used to looking sideways.

It seems that, with enlightenment, there can also be tremendous emphasis placed on the notion of oneness. Many have described a sense of ecstasy associated with feelings of connection to something eternal. Many will use hours of meditation to achieve this state. Some people have seizures that produce the sensation (and therefore resist treatment for their seizures). Some will bypass the meditation and use a "shortcut" via the use of hallucinogens. Indeed, I have read of users who will endure a dozen horribly bad trips just to re-experience this state.

What is so attractive about this state? Very possibly, it is a very pleasant balm to our fears of insignificance.

The shortcut bypasses the important work of enlightenment. There is no substitute for the practice of looking inward. We ought to want to discover the underlying beliefs that promote reflexive, counterproductive behavior. We don't want to clear our minds; we want to observe them. We ought to want to wrestle with the process of adopting more adaptive beliefs. Skipping ahead and basking in the sensation that we are one with the infinite may tempt us to think we are done. Why would we ever want to be done? It smacks too much of the wish to see oneself as perfect. It is better to strive to be humbler.

My notion of enlightenment is somewhat Eastern but also very Western. It is devoted to the idea that reason is the primary source of answers to our problems. I hope that we want truth to make sense; not just to "feel" it. Wherever possible, I have tried to bring science and reason to questions. This enables the changing of beliefs by answering important "why" questions. You can't refute the notion that a subjective, shame-based explanation for events is valid without them. On the other hand, when we understand human development and the workings of the brain, it is not at all difficult to establish useful, objective explanations for events.

I am devoted to *diminishing* suffering. Discomfort with self is the source of much suffering. Our belief in shame is the wellspring of our discomfort. We believe in shame because of our unchallenged expectation of perfection.

Shame leads to insecurity because we assume responsibility for the failures of our parents to meet our needs. We create a lineup of character suspects that we imagine to be responsible for their indifference. We then criticize ourselves in the hope that this will dispel the suspects while also seeking compensatory approval from others.

I have hoped to show that the suspects in our lineup are innocent. I have hoped to impeach shame and all of its minions. Without shame, we will no longer live in darkness.

I have hoped to establish the notion of the humble self-esteem. This is a much sounder idea than perpetually trying to achieve perfection; or trying to prove superiority; or trying to maintain a steady inflow of approval; or trying to maintain an illusion of perfection achieved. We are always imperfect. We are insignificant. We have no free will. Random chance rules our lives. We all have the same value. We are always playing the very best we can at every moment in time. When we know this, the tremendous energies devoted to questions of self-esteem are liberated for every other concern we may have.

I also have hoped to have established a way of living in comfort with our wishes and impulses. There is a rational case to be made for why weakness, anger, selfishness, grief and insecurity are states of mind we can experience with serenity.

I recognize that the title of this book could have seemed to be incredibly pretentious. Perhaps the voice in the wilderness can be excused of the wish to shout. In contrast to the title, I suppose the execution could be experienced as rather pedestrian; as homely as home-made socks.

Muhammad Ali said that if our dreams didn't scare us, they weren't big enough. The title of the book suggests a pretty big dream. But, with the humble self-esteem, we have nothing to fear. The ideas you found here are immune from pretention.

I hope you can embrace change. I hope you will come to feel that being "right" suggests stasis; that it is inconsistent with the humble self-esteem. And besides, the pilgrimage is too fun to just *stop* somewhere.

I want to tell a story of psychotherapy. It is an old Jewish parable. It's cool, because it gets all the elements right; long before there ever was psychotherapy. In the story, there is a prince who develops what we would call a psychotic break. He comes to believe he is a rooster. He takes off all of his clothes, gets under a table, and starts pecking around. His parents, the king and queen are, naturally, quite distressed. Many wise men are called in to help but, one by one, they fail.

Finally, an unheralded man appears (perhaps from the wilderness!) and claims to know what to do. He takes off all of his clothes and gets under the table. He starts pecking and scratching about, just like the prince. After a couple of weeks, he looks over at the prince and says, "Don't you think it's possible that we would still be chickens if we wore pants? Pants would be ever so much more comfortable, and practical too..."

And so, incrementally, the prince was cured. Almost everything in psychotherapy is contained in this story. The therapist has a belief that is a closer representation of reality and, if adopted, will lead to decreased suffering. He decreases fears of change by gaining the prince's trust. He decreases attachment to old ideas with rational arguments for how the prince will be better off. He uses empathy and avoids confrontation. And he uses *timing*. He knows when the time is right to introduce a new idea. He knows how to present the idea in a way that maximizes the chances it will be well received.

This book can do much of all this, except manage the timing. Maybe, if the timing has been not quite right for you, there will be a time in the future where it will be better.

On the other hand, this book has one thing that is hard to deliver in psychotherapy. In psychotherapy, the information comes out in little pieces. The patient can feel like the proverbial blind man, trying to understand an elephant. It can be hard to see how every piece connects to an integrated whole.

In the end, I recognize that it is still just an image of an elephant. There is much that could have embellished every chapter. I have hoped to distill, from an ocean of complexities, a version of the truth that is the most useful. Thomas Payne's "Common Sense" owed much of its influence to its brevity. I hope the same is true of my uncommon sense. If you are with me, the stage is set for you to flesh out the elephant on your own.

There is another important thing that happens in psychotherapy. The patient will tell me that it all, "sounds good up here" (point to head) but, "I don't feel it down here" (point to heart). In time, they come to the belief that I, at least, believe it. They believe that I'm not just saying it because that's what I was taught to say. They see that I made the leap from head to heart and that helps them make their leap.

Hopefully, you have had the sensation, while reading this, that I could understand you. Hopefully, you really get it that I wouldn't be judgmental. And, a lot of this is *my stuff!* I wasn't taught it. Of course, I believe it.

I sure hope you can make your jump!

There is so much suffering in the world. The murmur of it is all around. Collectively it has become a roar. It is so strange, this life of ours. We come into the world with an expectation that everything will be perfect and that expectation leads to the ruin of our dreams. Maybe I am only nostalgic, but it seems like things are getting worse.

I have hoped to ease your suffering. By now, it must be becoming clearer to you how profoundly we are influenced by instinct. I know it can be a humbling conclusion to reach. Yet, I have hoped that you (we) may wake from a long and vivid dream; that you may gain release from the shackles of instinct. The best that humans may become relies on this.

Life is a miracle. Your part in it is important. We live in times of peril. It is unclear how long we will be allowed to discover what we can become. It is a good time to start your pilgrimage.

Fortunately, there *is* a pilgrimage we can take that leads to a better place. It is a pilgrimage that we can take individually and collectively. As you go travelling, as long as I am able, I will always wish you the best.

Appendix

A review of suggested invalid beliefs that lead to automatic, maladaptive behaviors and the more adaptive alternative beliefs

***

Black-and-white thinking is desirable.
> Especially when dealing with our problems, more complexity is desirable.

Shame is a valid concept
> Shame is a mistaken interpretation of the disparity between instinct driven expectations and reality.

Humans can be perfect.
> Hardly.

Shame accounts for our imperfections.
> Imperfection is inevitable.

We feel shame.
> What we feel has been mislabeled. We feel horror.

We need shame to control ourselves.
> We have plenty of motives for self-control.
> Shame diminishes self-control.

Insecurity is shameful.
> Insecurity is inevitable and can be useful.

Mistakes are shameful.
> Mistakes are inevitable and can be useful.

We are responsible for our parent's feelings about us.
> Life events determined our parent's perspectives before we were born.

We were never capable of having much
influence on them.
We can make insecurity go away with enough
_____.

    We make primary insecurity go away
    when we eliminate our character suspects
    and challenge how we feel.
Certainty is desirable.

    Certainty leads to poor decisions and bad
    surprises.
We can learn about our worthiness from other
people.

    We learn about the behavior preferences of
    other people from other people. (and,
    potentially, many other things).
Selfishness is shameful.

    Selfishness is inevitable. We want to be
    wise with it. This requires that we like it.
Anger is shameful.

    Ditto.
Laziness is a valid concept.

    There is much objective complexity that
    explains any level of industry.
Different people have different value.

    Everybody has the same value. Luck
    explains the observable differences
    between people.
A person's value can change.

    A person's value never changes.
We have free will.

    Nope.

Popular opinion determines reality.

> Hopefully, evidence and reason determine reality.

Life is fair.

> Nope. Sorry.

When we have bad luck, we deserve compensatory good luck.

> That would be the most unlikely form of luck. Probably never happening.

Obesity is shameful.

> There is much objective complexity that explains a person's weight.

Diets work.

> Nope.

Addiction is shameful.

> There is much objective complexity that explains addiction behavior.

Boredom is bad.

> Boredom can be useful. We have been sadly acculturated to dislike our thoughts.

We should try to do all things well.

> We should wisely prioritize our efforts.

Competence imparts superiority.

> Competence is the product of luck.

Extreme competence is desirable.

> Extreme competence probably comes with too many costs.

We can settle our doubts about lovability by finding love.

> Unlikely and inefficient. It's better to look inward.

Sexual impulse is shameful.
>   We want to be wise with sexual impulses.
>   This requires that we like them.

Grief is shameful.
>   Oh, please.

It's strange that bad stuff happens to us.
>   Bad stuff is inevitable.

We aren't going to die.
>   Unlikely. We aren't that significant.

About the Author

Scott Elrod attended medical school and received his residency training in psychiatry at the University of Washington. He lives in Missoula, Montana with his wife. He has two children.

Made in the
USA
Columbia, SC